On Earth
As It Is in Heaven

Jews, Christians, and
Liberation Theology

RABBI DAN COHN-SHERBOK

ORBIS BOOKS

Maryknoll, New York 10545

The Catholic Foreign Mission Society of America (Maryknoll) recruits and trains people for overseas missionary service. Through Orbis Books Maryknoll aims to foster the international dialogue that is essential to mission. The books published, however, reflect the opinions of their authors and are not meant to represent the official position of the society.

"Pesach has Come to the Ghetto Again" by Binem Heller, which appears in *The Passover Anthology* by Philip Goodman, is copyrighted by and used through the courtesy of The Jewish Publication Society

Manuscript editor: Mary J. Heffron

Library of Congress Cataloging-in-Publication Data

Cohn-Sherbok, Dan.
 On earth as it is in heaven.

 Bibliography: p.
 1. Liberation theology. 2. Christianity and other
religions—Judaism. 3. Judaism—Relations—
Christianity. 4. Jesus Christ—Person and offices.
5. Kingdom of God. I. Title.
BT83.57.C63 1986 230 86-23509
ISBN 0-88344-410-0 (pbk.)

FOR LAVINIA AND DIGGER

Contents

Foreword

Attached to the ancient scriptures of the people of God is a slim volume, a collection of writings produced in the second half of the first century A.D. Those writings are in their different ways a commentary on the scriptures, provoked by the urgent need to understand the significance of Jesus of Nazareth. They cannot stand by themselves—indeed, as the history of Christian theology and practice has repeatedly shown, if they are referred to out of context they are often misunderstood and misleading.

As in the course of the last century Christians have become conscious again of being a pilgrim people among the nations and have begun to taste the consequence of being a minority in the world, so the scholastic rigidity of their theology has thawed and the churches' corporate worship and ethic have universally found the sources of renewal. Those sources are of course in the scriptures, which Christians hold in common with the Jews, and not only in the scriptures but in the whole cast of mind, the perspective on God, the world, and human beings, which for short is designated Hebrew and biblical.

So far this process has been largely internal within the churches: the old apologetic, not to say polemics, between Christians and Jews has hardly as yet modulated into dialogue, though there have been long-standing friendships between individuals, some important ones indeed in earlier times. And there have been groups of Jewish and Christian scholars, such as the London Society for the Study of Religion, founded eighty years ago by Claude Montefiore and Baron von Hügel, and the Rainbow Group in Jerusalem. The consequent developments in theology and liturgy have been well charted.

Not so in the field of ethics. The great value of *Jews, Christians, and Liberation Theology* is that in it Rabbi Dan Cohn-Sherbok shows both how the prophetic tradition of Israel has surfaced in the church's struggle in the third world and how that tradition in its understanding of the kingdom of God enables Jews and Christians to find common theological ground in thought and practice. The implications of this approach are far-reaching. Christians have generally found it easier to assimilate the prophetic strand of the Bible than to come to terms with the law fundamental to Jewish faith. It may be that in reflecting on Jesus' prayer "Thy kingdom come, thy will be done on earth as it is in heaven" (the text, as it were, of this book), Christians will come to understand more fully the integrity of the Jewish understanding of God's dealings with creation. It may be also that Jews, by reflecting on those aspects of their tradition reemphasized by liberation theology, will be enabled more fully to engage in their ancient commission as God's people.

Is it too much to pray that if reflection can be common, the oldest wounds may in God's providence be healed?

VICTOR DE WAAL
Dean of Canterbury

INTRODUCTION

A New Approach to Jewish-Christian Dialogue

1. OBSTACLES TO DIALOGUE

For nineteen centuries Jews and Christians have lived alongside one another; nevertheless positive dialogue between these two faiths has only recently taken place. During the first Christian centuries each side expressed fierce hostility toward the other. In the Acts of the Apostles, for example, we are told that Stephen became the first Christian martyr when he was stoned to death by the Jews for his faith in the heavenly Son of Man (Acts 7:54–60). Similar antipathy was reflected in rabbinic sources such as the Jerusalem Talmud where we read: "When Nebuchadnezzar used the expression 'He is like a son of the gods' (Daniel 3:25) an angel came down from heaven, smote him on the mouth and said, 'Blasphemer! Does God have a son?' " (T.J. Shabbat, 8). The same antagonistic attitude was deeply rooted in the writings of the early church. Origen, for example, argued, "We may thus assert that the Jews will not return to their earlier situation, for they have committed the most abominable of crimes in forming this conspiracy against the saviour of the human race" (*Contra Celsum*, 4, 23). In other words, Origen was maintaining that God punished the Jews because of their rejection of Jesus.

This enmity continued all through the Middle Ages and it eventu-

1

ally gave rise to a number of religious debates. During the course of a disputation in Barcelona in 1263, the king of Aragon posed the following questions to Rabbi Moses Nahmanides: "Has the Messiah already appeared? Is the Messiah promised by the prophets a human or divine figure? Who holds the correct faith, the Christians or the Jews?" In reply to the first question Nahmanides argued that the promises in the Old Testament for the messianic age had not yet been fulfilled: war, bloodshed, injustice, and outrage still held sway on the earth. He also argued that Jesus had not freed human beings from the guilt of original sin since the punishments decreed by God for the sin of the first human being (according to Christian doctrine) remained in force. In answer to the second question, Nahmanides replied that in the Jewish tradition the Messiah was to be human rather than divine. And finally, in answer to the third question, he declared that Christian doctrine was fundamentally unreasonable and therefore could not be true (Schoeps 1963, 55–56).

Other Jewish responses to such questions can be found in medieval rabbinic writings. Saadya Gaon, for example, in *The Book of Beliefs and Opinions* argued that Christianity was a human creation falsely maintaining that it was divinely revealed (Gaon 1948). In *The Kuzari* Jehudah Halevi similarly maintained that Christianity professed false doctrines which distorted divine truth (Halevi [1927] 1964). Isaac Troki, in *Faith Strengthened*, attempted to show that christological interpretations of the Old Testament had no solid foundation (Troki 1975).

It was not until the seventeenth century, in a debate between the Christian Phillip van Limborch and the Jew Isaac Orbio de Castro, that Jews and Christians showed some measure of tolerance for each other; yet even then neither protagonist had a sympathetic understanding of the other's faith. Orbio, on the one hand, stated that it was a mistake to read christological notions into the Old Testament. Limborch, on the other, argued that Jesus was greater than Moses and that it was necessary to have faith in Jesus Christ in order to achieve salvation (Schoeps 1963, 55–56).

In the eighteenth century the dialogue between Moses Mendelssohn and Johann Caspar Lavater showed a similar lack of mutual understanding despite Mendelssohn's belief that Christianity was, in some respects, true. On the basis of a rejection of the christological interpretation of passages in the Old Testament, he attempted to demonstrate the irrationality of the doctrines of the Trinity, the incarnation, the resurrection, the ascension, and the redemption wrought through Jesus (see Jacobs 1974, 15–23).

In the following century other Jewish thinkers discussed the relationship between Judaism and Christianity. Salomon Form-stecher, for example, in *Die Religion des Geistes*, argued that Judaism was the true world religion, whereas Christianity was disguised paganism (Formstecher 1841). Similarly, in *Revelation according to the Doctrine of the Synagogue*, Salomon Ludwig Steinham declared that Christianity was a mixture of Jewish and pagan ideas and alleged that the doctrine of the incarnation was self-contradictory (Steinham 1863).

There have been similar conflicts in this century. The discussion between Martin Buber and Karl Ludwig Schmidt highlighted theological differences between Judaism and Christianity. At the beginning of the debate, Schmidt proposed:

> The only important question is whether nearly two thousand years ago the Jewish nation, the Jewish Church of the time, did not harden their hearts against the Messiah sent by God, thereupon, through the destruction of Jerusalem, losing the focus of their ramified Diaspora, and thenceforth living in the Diaspora, in dispersion, without a spiritual centre [Schoeps 1963, 55–56].

In response Buber stated:

> We cannot ascribe finality to any one of His [God's] revelations, nor to any one [revelation] the character of the Incarnation. Unconditionally, that futuristic World of the Lord points to the Beyond at every moment of passing time; God transcends absolutely all of His manifestations [Schoeps 1963, 151].

Recently some Jewish writers have discussed Jewish-Christian relations in the light of the Holocaust. Richard Rubenstein, for example, in *After Auschwitz*, maintains that Jews and Christians can develop personal relationships only when there exists theological ambiguity and uncertainty. He writes:

> When the Jew holds firmly to the doctrine of the election of Israel and the Torah as the sole content of God's revelation to mankind, the Christian insistence upon the decisive character of the Christ event in human history must be, at best, error and, at worst, blasphemy.

Further, he continues, when the Christian

> is convinced that the divine-human encounters recorded in Scripture find their true meaning and fulfillment in the Cross, Jews are at best the blind who cannot see; at worst, they are the demonic perverters, destroyers and betrayers of mankind's true hope for salvation [Rubenstein 1966, 75].

Historically then, it can be seen that the central obstacle to real Jewish-Christian dialogue has been the clash of religious claims. In the *Jewish-Christian Argument*, H.J. Schoeps explains:

> During the first Centuries, the Jewish side had no other interest besides refuting Christian re-interpretations of Jewish doctrines, holding themselves aloof from true encounter through "refutations" of their opponents. When Christianity acceded to power, Christians no longer had any serious desire to engage in discussion with the Jews for the latter's very impotence was seen as an overwhelming instance of God's punishment. Within the intellectual arena of medieval scholasticism, Jews and Christians could properly have only the concern of justifying their own religion while, at the same time, flatly refusing to acknowledge the other's claim to truth [Schoeps 1963, 124].

There has been more scope for understanding in the modern period, but in fact, Jews and Christians have continued to emphasize the theological gulf that separates their faiths.

Thus, as a result of centuries of religious conflict and enmity, Jews have felt and continue to feel suspicion and distaste for both

Christians and Christianity. Recently further wounds have been inflicted by the Christian community. The Holocaust is not easily forgotten; the churches did not rise in a body to denounce Hitler's activities; the railway lines to Auschwitz were not bombed by the Allies. There is not much Christian interest in the plight of Jews in the Soviet Union; the much vaunted statement on Jewish innocence for the crucifixion is mild and was only achieved after much argument; and Christian criticism of the political and military activity of the State of Israel is common. Against this background the position of many Jews is understandable. Real dialogue is impossible in conditions of mutual distrust. Nearly two thousand years of being despised and persecuted have left their mark on the Jewish community.

2. NEW DIRECTIONS IN DIALOGUE

In spite of all this, the gulf between Christians and Jews seems to be narrowing and for several important reasons. First, as Walter Jacobs notes in *Christianity through Jewish Eyes*, scholarly exploration is increasing into the background of the New Testament (Jacobs 1974, 231). Jesus and Paul were Jewish figures. They kept the Jewish law; they participated in Jewish feasts. The pioneering work in this area done by such scholars as Samuel Sandmel, H.J. Schoeps (1961) and Geza Vermes has aroused much critical interest from both Christians and Jews. Quite apart from broadening the Christian understanding of their own religious background, these works also counterbalance the anti-Semitic elements of the New Testament.

Secondly, fruitful Jewish-Christian encounter seems to be more of a possibility today because it is being conducted on a personal level. In the last century the Jewish scholar Franz Rosenzweig carried on a long correspondence with his friend Ehrenberg, who was a Jewish convert to Christianity. Both men were intensely religious, but besides their faith, they brought friendship to their discussions. Rosenzweig wrote:

The truth, the entire truth, belongs neither to them nor to us. We (the Jews) bear it within ourselves, precisely, therefore, we must first gaze within ourselves if we wish to see it. So we will see the star, but not its rays. To encompass the whole truth one must not only see the light, but also what it illumines. They (the Christians) on the other hand, have been eternally destined to see the illumined object, but not the light. Thus though Christians and Jews see the truth in different ways, before God there is only one truth [Rozenzweig 1930, 3: 200 ff; see Jacobs 1974, 126].

This attempt to show the fundamental unity between the two religions (the first real Jewish recognition of the truth of Christianity) was conducted in a spirit of true friendship. Fortunately in this century similar encounters between Jews and Christians have been and continue to be undertaken in friendship and understanding in Israel, Europe, and the United States. Moreover, such amicable dialogue has resulted in the formation of numerous associations of Jews and Christians throughout the world.

The final factor contributing to interfaith encounter concerns a significant theological development within the church. In the past the doctrine of the incarnation was a central obstacle to authentic dialogue between Jews and Christians. But today within Christianity itself there is serious disagreement about the doctrine. In *God and the Universe of Faiths* John Hick makes it clear that a growing number of Christians, both professional theologians and lay people, refuse to understand the traditional doctrine of the incarnation literally. The incarnation, Hick maintains, is a "mythological idea." As such, he writes:

it cannot literally apply to Jesus. But as a poetic image— which is powerfully evocative even though it conveys no literal meaning—it expresses the religious significance of Jesus in a way that has proved effective for nearly two millennia [Hick 1975, 172].

Given this radical change in the understanding of the nature of Jesus, liberal Christians can no longer condemn the Jew for refusing to accept that Jesus was literally, "God of God, Light of Light, Very God of Very God, Begotten not made, being of One Substance with the Father," since that is exactly what they are doing themselves.

3. JUDAISM AND LIBERATION THEOLOGY

Christian-Jewish dialogue has thus ceased to be the impossibility it once was. But there is another cause for hope, and it has as yet remained unexplored. In Latin America, as well as in other countries in the third world, a new Christian theological development has been taking place in the last few decades. Liberation theology, as it is frequently called, has captured the imagination of Roman Catholics and Protestants. Combining theory with practice, this movement attempts to use the insights of Marxist social criticism to forge a new vision of the Christian message. Most importantly for Jewish-Christian encounter, liberation theologians have gone back to their Jewish roots in the Old Testament. Suddenly Jewish and Christian writers find themselves using the same vocabulary and motifs, and this bond paves the way for a mutual examination of commonly shared religious ideals.

For third world theologians, the biblical account portrays the Israelites as an oppressed people. Suffering torment, their complaints led to new burdens rather than to relief (Ex 1:8-14). But the Israelites were not alone: God heard the groaning of the people and remembered the covenant (Ex 2:23-25). Moreover, God declared that the people would be liberated from their bondage. Moses was delegated to lead the people out of Egypt, and after many trials, this was accomplished (Ex 3:7-10).

This story of hope has inspired the oppressed in third world countries, particularly in Latin America. It is of solace to hear that God does not remain aloof from situations of human history, that God acted against Pharaoh, and that Israel's liberation was not simply from individual sin and guilt; Israel's freedom meant liberation from oppressive political and economic structures. It is clear that God has a real concern with life on earth.

This account shows that God is a living God and that God takes sides with the downtrodden. This means that God is against the Pharaohs of this world, the modern exploiters. And who, Robert Brown asks, are the Pharaohs of the world today? It is not difficult to identify them, he writes:

They are the tiny minority at home who are in collusion against the great majority; they are the churches and the churchpersons who give support to such oligarchies; and they are the rich and powerful from other nations who keep national oligarchies in power, thereby becoming complicit in the ongoing exploitation of the poor [Brown 1978, 89–90].

Liberation theologians emphasize the scriptural message that God demands justice. This theme is found throughout the prophetic books of the Bible, and is illustrated by numerous textual references. J.P. Miranda, for example, in *Marx and the Bible*, cites the words of Jeremiah (22:13–15):

> Shame on the man who builds his house by non-justice,
> and completes its upstairs rooms by non-right,
> who makes his fellow man work for nothing,
> without paying him his wages,
> who says, "I will build myself an imposing palace
> with spacious rooms upstairs,"
> who sets windows in it,
> panels it with cedar, and paints it vermilion
> [Miranda 1974, 44].

Referring to the practice of justice and right, and the defence of the poor, Jeremiah posed the question: "Is not that what it means to know me?—it is Yahweh who speaks" (Jer 22:16).

In this rhetorical question Jeremiah explained that knowing God entailed acts of righteousness. To know God was not to engage in ritual acts nor to subscribe to correct religious beliefs. To know God was to do justice. This conviction added depth to a later passage in Jeremiah in which God's new covenant was described. In this covenant "there will be no further need for neighbor to try to teach neighbor, or brother to say to brother, 'Learn to know Yahweh!' No, they will all know me" (Jer 31:34). Here an explicit equation was made between knowing God and doing justice, which transforms the nature of the new covenant.[1]

Not only, according to liberation theologians, is the knowledge of God predicated on doing justice, but the worship of God also entails acts of righteousness. In this regard Miranda quotes the words of Amos (5.21, 23–24) to emphasize that without justice there can be no true cultic worship:

I hate, I despise your feasts,
and I take no delight in your solemn assemblies. . . .
Take away from me the noise of your songs;
to the melody of your harps I will not listen.
But let justice roll down like waters,
and righteousness like a mighty stream
                    [Miranda 1974, 44; in Brown 1978, 92].

Such convictions, based on Scripture, have had a profound effect on the personal lives of liberation theologians. The Colombian priest Camilo Torres, for example, stopped exercising his priestly duties because he felt they kept him from identifying with those who were trying to establish a more just society:

I have ceased to say Mass [in order] to practice love for people in temporal, economic and social spheres. When the people have nothing against me, when they have carried out the revolution, then I will return to offering Mass, God willing. I think that in this way I follow Christ's injunction "leave thy gift upon the altar and go first to be reconciled to thy brothers (and sisters)" [in Brown 1978, 93].

Such an attitude was summarized by Isaiah in a passage in which appropriate forms of worship were described. God explained that fasting had made the people quarrel among themselves and oppress their workers; this was not what God desired:

Is not this what I require of you as a fast—
to loose the fetters of injustice,
to untie the knots of the yoke,
to snap every yoke
and set free those who have been crushed?
Is it not sharing your food with the hungry,
taking the homeless poor into your home,
clothing the naked when you meet them
and never evading a duty to your kinsfolk? [Isa 58:6–7].

It is clear to liberation theologians that their message will in all likelihood not be accepted by the established churches. Rather, drawing upon the biblical concept of a saving remnant, they see themselves as a minority within the body of Christ. Theirs is not an attitude of despair; it is consonant with the prophetic role. In 760 B.C. when Amos inveighed against evil and cultic corruption, he told the ancient Israelites to "hate evil, and love good, and establish justice within the gate." Yet the most he promised was that "it may be that the Lord, the God of hosts, will be gracious to the remnant of Joseph" (Am 5:15).

This should not however result in an elitist attitude. Rather, as J. Ratzinger points out in *Le Nouveau Peuple de Dieu*, the remnant has an obligation to others:

> God does not divide humanity (the "many" and the "few") to save the few and hurl the many into perdition. Nor does he do it to save the many in an easy way and the few in a hard way. Instead we could say that he uses the numerical few as a leverage point for raising up the many [in Brown 1978, 160].

Embodying this message of liberation, the church is to be, in the words of Helder Camara, "the Abrahamic minority." Abraham was the one who obeyed God and travelled to new and unexplored places. Camara explains:

> Everywhere there are minorities capable of understanding Action for Justice and Peace and adopting it as a workshop for study and action. Let us call these minorities the Abrahamic minorities, because like Abraham, we are hoping against all hope [Camara 1976, 69].

This Abrahamic minority will hear the cries of the oppressed; it will be committed to "the most important task in our century: to free those two out of three who are still in slavery, even though they are no longer called slaves" (Camara 1976, 21).

In this Christian message it is obvious that liberation theologians have relied heavily on the central biblical themes of freedom from oppression, justice, and the role of the saving remnant. Utilizing Pentateuchal and prophetic imagery and symbolism, they have explored the role of the church in contemporary society and have revitalized and readapted the teachings of the Old Testament. This return to scriptural sources serves as a bridge between Judaism and Christianity. Although Jews cannot accept any christological doctrines embedded in the exposition of this message, they can recognize much common ground. These are particularly important links in the modern world where the rich and the poor live side by side. In the light of this return to Jewish sources, it is now possible for both faiths to work together in trust and hope. Such a joint project is far removed from those centuries of mistrust and persecution in which Jews and Christians regarded one another with contempt and hostility.

In this study I shall first show how Judaism differs from traditional Christianity. Of course one cannot do full justice to the complexities of the development of Jewish and Christian theology through the centuries. Nevertheless it is possible to chart certain emphases within the two traditions that give rise to a general pattern of divergence. In subsequent chapters I shall illustrate the ways in which Christian liberation theologians have redefined a number of central religious concepts in Christianity and brought them more in line with the Jewish tradition. Finally, I shall explain on the basis of this common ground how Jews and Christians can become partners in a mutual quest for the liberation of those who are oppressed and persecuted.

CHAPTER ONE

Judaism and Christianity: Their Differences

1. DOCTRINE OF GOD

For most Jews the central difference between Judaism and Christianity concerns the doctrine of God.[1] For over two thousand years Jews have daily recited the *Shema*: "Hear O Israel: the Lord our God is one Lord" (Dt 6:4). Jewish children are taught this verse as soon as they can speak, and it is recited at their deathbed. Jewish martyrs proclaimed these words as they gave up their lives. Throughout the ages it has been the most important declaration in the Jewish faith. In making this statement the Jews attest to their belief that there is only one God and that God is indivisible. God is an absolute unity who cannot be syncretistically linked with other gods. In addition, since the word "one" in Hebrew (*echad*) also means "unique," Jews imply that God is different from anything else that is worshipped; only God possesses divinity. Nothing can be compared to God: "To whom then will ye liken me that I should be equal?" (Is 40:25). Thus Jewish monotheism denies the existence of any other divine being; there is only one supreme being who is Lord of all.

Among medieval Jewish theologians the doctrine of God's unity embraced the idea that there is no plurality in God's being; God is absolute simplicity: (*"pashut be-takhlit ha-peshitut"*) (Jacobs

1973, 27). This doctrine of God's unity meant for many medieval theologians the purification of the concept of God so as to remove any notion of multiplicity. The great medieval philosopher Maimonides, for example, argued that

> This God is One, not two or more than two, but One whose unity is different from all other unities that there are. . . . Nor is He one as a body, containing parts and dimensions. . . . But His is a unity than which there is no other anywhere [*Yad, Yesode Ha-Torah* 1:7].

A classic formulation of this view was contained in *The Kingly Crown* by the medieval poet Ibn Gabriol:

> Thou art One, the beginning of all computation, the base of all construction.
> Thou art One, and in the mystery of Thy Oneness the wise of heart are astonished, for they know not what it is.
> Thou art One, but not as the one that is counted or owned, for number and chance cannot reach thee, nor attribute, nor form.
> Thou art One, but my mind is too feeble to set Thee a law or a limit, and therefore I say: "I will take heed to my ways, that I sin not with my tongue."
> Thou art One and Thou art exalted above abasement and falling—not like a man, who falls when he is alone [in Jacobs 1973, 28].

Given this understanding of God it is not surprising that in the early rabbinic period Christianity was attacked for its doctrine of the Incarnation. According to rabbinic sources, the belief that God was in Christ was heretical; the doctrine that God is both Father and Son was viewed as a dualistic theology. For this reason there were no early rabbinic polemics against the Trinity. Rather the Incarnation was criticized, especially in Caesarea in the third century, when rabbis were in contact with Christians. The third century scholar R. Abahu commented on Numbers 23:19:

God is not a man, that He should lie; neither the son of man, that He should repent: hath He said, and shall He not do it? Or hath He spoken and shall He not make it good?

R. Abahu interpreted the last part of this verse not as a question but as a statement and the pronoun in the first part of the verse as referring not to God but to humanity. Thus he said,

If a man says to you, "I am a god," he is lying; "I am the Son of Man," he will end up being sorry for it; "I am going up to Heaven," he will not fulfil what he has said [J. Talmud Taan 2:1].

In the Middle Ages the doctrine of the Trinity was bitterly denounced as well. Christian exegetes in this period interpreted the *Shema*, with its three references to God, as referring to the Trinity (see *Jewish Encyclopaedia*, 12:261). Jewish exegetes maintained that in this prayer there is reference only to one God and not three persons in the Godhead. Christians often asserted that Jewish polemics against the Trinity were based on an inadequate understanding (see Jacobs 1973, 26). Although it is true that some of these criticisms were uninformed, all Jewish thinkers rejected trinitarianism as incompatible with monotheism. Jewish martyrs in the Middle Ages gave their lives rather than accept such a doctrine. Modern Jewish thought is equally critical of any attempt to harmonize the belief in God's unity with the doctrine of a triune God. Contemporary Jewish theologians of all degrees of observance affirm that Judaism is fundamentally incompatable with what they perceive as the polytheistic character of trinitarian belief.

2. JESUS

Connected with the Jewish rejection of the doctrines of the Incarnation and the Trinity, Jews have consistently denied the Christian claim that Jesus is the Messiah. The term "Messiah" comes from the Hebrew root *mashiah* and means "the anointed one." In the Bible this term originally referred to any person anointed with sacred oil for the purpose of holding a high office, such as a king or high priest. In certain contexts it was applied to any person for whom God had a special purpose, as, for example, Cyrus, the king of Persia (see Is 45:1). Some prophets foresaw the coming of a personal redeemer of the house of David, whereas others spoke of a Messianic Age. Eventually these biblical ideas were elaborated in the Apocrypha and Pseudepigrapha, and thus a complicated fabirc of messianic speculation was formed (see Klausner 1956; Patai 1979).

In rabbinic literature the order of redemption was outlined as follows: (1) the signs of the Messiah; (2) the birth pangs of the Messiah; (3) the coming of Elijah; (4) the trumpet of the Messiah; (5) the ingathering of the exiles; (6) the reception of proselytes; (7) the war with Gog and Magog; (8) the Days of the Messiah; (9) the renovation of the world; (10) the Day of Judgment; (11) the resurrection of the dead; (12) the world to come. All these elements have been discussed in rabbinic sources as well as in medieval and modern Jewish literature (see Jacobs 1973, 294).

On the basis of their doctrine of the advent of the Messiah, Jews refuse to accept Jesus as their Messiah and Savior for a number of important reasons. First, according to Judaism it is obvious that Jesus did not fulfil the messianic expectations. Jesus did not restore the kingdom of David to its former glory; nor did he gather in the dispersed ones of Israel and restore all the laws of the Torah that were in abeyance (such as the sacrifical cult). He did not compel all Israel to walk in the way of the Torah nor did he rebuild the Temple and usher in a new order in the world and nature.

In other words, Jesus did not inaugurate a cataclysmic change in history. Universal peace, in which there is neither war nor competition, did not come about on earth. Thus for Jews Jesus did not fulfil the prophetic messianic hope in a redeemer who would bring political and spiritual redemption as well as earthly blessings and moral perfection to the human race.

A second objection to Jesus concerns the Christian claim that he possesses a special relationship with God. This notion was repeatedly stated in the gospels. In Matthew, for example, we read: "No one knows the Son except the Father; and no one knows the Father, except the Son" (11:27). In John's Gospel Jesus declares: "I am the way, and the truth, and the life; no one comes to the Father but by me. If you had known me, you would have known my Father also; henceforth you have known him and have seen him (14:6–7). This concept undermined the Jewish conviction that God is equally near to all.

The third objection to Jesus arises from his attitude toward sin and sinners. The traditional task of the prophets was to castigate Israel for rejecting God's law, not to forgive sin. Jesus however took upon himself the power to do this. Thus he declared with regard to a paralytic: "For which is easier, to say, 'Your sins are forgiven' or to say, 'Rise and walk'? But that you may know that the Son of man has authority on earth to forgive sins"—he then said to the paralytic—"Rise, take up your bed and go home" (Mt 9:5–6). When Jesus said to a woman of ill-repute "Your sins are forgiven" his companions were shocked. "Who is this, who even forgives sins?" they asked (Lk 7:48–49). It is not surprising that this was their reaction since such a usurpation of God's perogative was without precedent. A similar objection applies to the gospel record that Jesus performed miracles on his own authority without making reference to God (Jn 5:18–21).

A fourth objection to Jesus concerns his otherworldliness. The rabbis sought to provide adequate social legislation, but Jesus had a view different from theirs. To him poverty was not a deprivation; on the contrary, he regarded it as meritorious. For example, Jesus told a potential disciple: "If you would be perfect, go, sell what you possess and give to the poor, and you will have treasure in heaven; and come follow me" (Mt 19:21). In the Sermon on the Mount, Jesus proclaimed: "Blessed are you poor, for yours is the kingdom of God" (Lk 6:20). In Jewish eyes, however, poverty was an evil; the sages sought to alleviate it by enacting laws to tax the wealthy for the benefit of the poor.

A further objection to Jesus concerns his admonition to break all human ties: "Whoever of you does not renounce all that he has cannot be my disciple" (Lk 14:33). Or again, "Who is my mother?, and who are my brothers? . . . Here are my mother and my brothers! For whoever does the will of my Father in heaven is my brother, and sister, and mother" (Mt 12:48–50). Similarly, he declared: "Call no man your father on earth, for you have one Father, who is in heaven" (Mt 23:9). In contrast to these views, Judaism asserted that persons could not live a full life unless they were members of a family and were well integrated into the larger community. The renunciation of family bonds was regarded as a travesty of the created order.

Finally, Jesus' teaching is rejected by Jews because his interpretation of Jewish law is at variance with rabbinic tradition. Though at one point in the gospels Jesus declared that no change should be made in the law (Mt 5:17), he disregarded a number of important precepts. Several times on the Sabbath, for example, Jesus cured individuals who were not dangerously ill, in violation of the rabbinic precept that the Sabbath law can only be broken for the saving and preserving of life (Mt 12:9–14; Lk 13:10–16; 14:3–6). Conversely, Jesus was more strict about the law of divorce than the Pharisees. Thus he stated:

> It was also said, "Whoever divorces his wife, let him give her a certificate of divorce." But I say to you that every one who divorces his wife, except on the ground of unchastity, makes her an adultress; and whoever marries a divorced woman commits adultery [Mt. 5:31f.]

In a similar vein Jesus rejected the biblical and rabbinic teaching regarding dietary laws: "Not that which entereth into the mouth defileth the man," he stated, "but what comes out of the mouth, this defiles a man" (Mt 15:11).

Another serious divergence from traditional Jewish law was Jesus' view that the ritual washing of hands before meals was unimportant. In response to the Pharisees' criticism of his disciples for eating without first washing their hands, he rebuked the Pharisees for not keeping the ethical commandments; "These are," he stated, "what defiles a man: but to eat with unwashed hands does not defile man" (Mt 15:20).

Jesus also violated the laws regarding fasts. The gospels record that when the Pharisees were fasting Jesus' disciples did not fast. When questioned about this, he replied: "Can the wedding guests mourn as long as the bridegroom is with them? The days will come, when the bridegroom is taken away from them, and then they will fast" (Mt 9:15). When the Pharisees criticized the disciples for plucking wheat on the Sabbath, Jesus proclaimed: "The Son of man is lord of the sabbath" (Mt 12:8).

3. THE LAW

Jesus' rejection of Jewish law served as the basis for Christianity's repudiation of its legal inheritance. Possibly the most forceful dismissal of the legal system was presented in Jesus' parables of the old and new. These parables were replies to the question of why he and his disciples failed to keep a rabbinically binding fast:

> No one sews a piece of unshrunk cloth on an old garment; if he does, the patch tears away from it, the new from the old, and a worse tear is made. And no one puts new wine into old wineskins; if he does, the wine will burst the skins, and the wine is lost, and so are the skins; but new wine is for fresh skins [Mk. 2:21–22].

This attitude was developed at length by Paul, who stated that the era of the Law was at an end. For Paul, the Law obstructed the spreading of the gospel; he therefore compared the slavery of those who lived under the Law with the freedom of those who believed in Jesus (Gal 2:4). According to Pauline theology, Christ was the end of the Law (Rom 10:4). Merely by doing what the Law commanded no one could be made upright. Such a view was consistent with the conviction that Jesus did not die in vain: "If justification were through the law, then Christ died to no purpose" (Gal 2:21). No compromise between faith and law was possible. The Law could only make human beings conscious of sin (Rom 3:20). Thus Paul wrote:

> If it had not been for the law, I should not have known sin. I should not have known what it is to covet if the law had not said, "You shall not covet." But sin, finding opportunity in the commandment, wrought in me all kinds of covetousness. Apart from the law sin lies dead [Rom 7:7–8].

This view of the Law inevitably divided Judaism from Christianity. From the time of Paul to the present day, Christians have seen the Law as an institution that makes persons conscious of sin without offering them salvation; the Law is understood as a force of compulsion and slavery in contrast to Christian love. But for Jews from Old Testament times to the modern period, the Law was viewed as a blessing from God.

The precepts of the Lord are right, rejoicing the heart [Ps 19:8].

The law of thy mouth is better to me
than thousands of gold and silver pieces [Ps 119:72].

I rejoice at Thy word
Like one who finds great spoil.
I hate and abhor falsehood,
but I love thy law.
Seven times a day I praise thee,
for thy righteous ordinances [Ps 119:162–164].

Christianity denies the Torah just those qualities Jews extol: the Law is Israel's beauty, sweetness, and strength. According to the rabbinic commentary on the Song of Songs, the Law was to be adored. On the verse "Thou art beautiful my love" (1:15) the Midrash commented:

The Law is beautiful through the commandments, both positive and negative, beautiful through loving deeds, beautiful in the Law of circumcision, beautiful in prayer, in the reading of the Shema, . . . beautiful, too, in repentance and in good works: beautiful in this world and beautiful in the world to come [Song of Songs R. 15.1 on 15;f. 126].

According to the Midrash, the words of the Law were secret and delightful: "A heap of wheat fenced with lilies" (Song 7:2). People hedge their fields and vineyards with thorns and brambles. But the words of the Torah are soft and gentle (Pes. R 35b imit.). Through the Torah one gained strength. R. Samuel b. Nahmani declared:

The words of the Law are compared to wine. For as wine strengthens, so the Law strengthens those who toil in it with all their will, as it is said, "The praises of God in their mouths, and a two-edged sword in their hands" (Ps 149:6) [Pes.K 102 a fin.—102b imit.].

Thus Christians from the earliest period to the present day have viewed the Law as something to be overcome, but Jews have regarded it as God's revelation for all time. Christian objection to the Law is rejected by Judaism, which sees the Torah as an expression of God's love for the chosen people. Unlike Christianity, which considers love the highest principle, Judaism maintains that subjective feeling is not sufficient to regulate human behavior; justice must be ensured by the intervention of Law.

The Law therefore is not, as Christians have insisted, a curse; it is a blessing.

Judaism holds that ethics and morality are safeguarded by the Law. . . . Christianity adheres to the view that the Law is a force of darkness in opposition to the new Christian light of faith and love. As a result, there is virtually no book in the multitude of volumes by Christian theologians treating the problems of the Law which does not stress, in one form or another, sometimes with more restraint and sometimes with less, that there is an inherent contradiction between obedience to the Law and genuine religiousness, a point which Jews will never concede [Weiss-Rosmarin 1965, 94].

The Law is fundamental to the Jew's faith; for this reason Jews declare daily in the liturgy: "I believe with perfect faith that his Torah will never be changed and that the Creator, blessed be his name, will never give us another Torah."[2]

4. FREE WILL, SIN, AND ATONEMENT

The Jewish view of the Law is predicated on the assumption that human beings have free will. Thus God declared: "I have set before thee this day life and good and death and evil, in that I command thee this day to love the Lord thy God, to walk in his ways" (Dt 30:15). Jews are free to act contrary to God's Law, as the rabbis stated:

> One should not say: "I cannot eat pork; I cannot enter into a forbidden sexual relation." Instead one should say, "I could act thus, but how may I do so against the command of my Father in Heaven" [Sifra to Lev. 20.26].

According to this principle, persons do what is in their power to do by their choice and will (Maimonides, *Guide for the Perplexed,* III, 17).

In Judaism this ethical freedom serves as the basis for law and ethics; human beings are rewarded or punished on the basis of their choices. Like Judaism, Christianity maintains that we have free will; yet Christianity asserts that we cannot liberate ourselves by our own effort. In Judaism, sinful human nature is also recognized; the evil inclination (*yetzer ha-ra*) is viewed as powerful and real. Yet Jews have always maintained that one can by oneself conquer sin. Throughout the Talmud, in medieval sources and in modern Jewish theology, it is stressed that human beings can successfully control their passions. The human soul was created pure and without blemish; our hope should be that at death we may be as free from sin as we were at birth (J. Talmud, Berachoth 4d). Unlike Christians Jews are to regard themselves as stronger than sin; even when they give in to an evil inclination, they still know that if they try hard enough, they can ultimately overcome temptation.

This conviction has important implications for the Jewish understanding of atonement. For Christians, however, human beings are by their very nature immersed in sin and guilt. "For I do not do the good I want, but the evil I do not want is what I do" (Rom 7:19). Atonement is only possible through the saving act of grace supplied by Christ's death. According to Christianity God's only Son was sacrificed to atone for the sins of humankind. Thus only by accepting and acknowledging that Christ died for their sins are Christians able to gain forgiveness.

Such a doctrine is irreconcilable with the Jewish concept of personal atonement. The Old Testament shows a gradual recognition that human beings were punished for their own sins. In particular the idea of personal responsibility was elaborated by the prophets. Jeremiah, for example, proclaimed: "Every one shall die for his own sin" (31:30). Throughout rabbinic literature and in modern Jewish theology the idea that each person must ask God to be forgiven is repeatedly expressed (see Jacobs 1973, 248–259). The sinner cannot rely on anyone else's taking the blame.

In the light of this understanding of repentance, Judaism stresses the importance of drawing near to God; mediation is not necessary since each person has equal access to the Divine. Indeed the rabbis pointed out that even priests have no power to bless; blessing comes from God and the priesthood only serves as God's mouthpiece (Bamidbar Rabbah XI, 8). As with blessing, so with forgiveness. Sinners require no outside help; all that is needed is for them to turn from their evil ways and practice righteousness. "To the Jew the subject of reconciliation with God presents no doctrinal difficulty. He holds that however many and gross his sins may be, he has only to repent sincerely" (Williams 1939, 159; in Weiss-Rosmarin 1965, 59).

5. ASCETICISM AND SOCIAL RESPONSIBILITY

In connection with the doctrine of sin, Christianity distinguishes between "spirit" and "flesh." Consequently, celibacy is extolled. "To the unmarried and the widows I say that it is well for them to remain single as I do. But if they cannot exercise self-control, they should marry. For it is better to marry than to be aflame with passion" (1 Cor 7:8–9). By contrast Judaism does not ascribe to the view that there is an unbridgeable gap between flesh and spirit. Rather it places the physical on an equal basis with the spiritual. Humankind's physical nature is viewed as part of God's creation; matter and spirit are inextricably linked in a harmonious relation. For Jews the needs of the body are spiritualized. For this reason the rabbis stated that in the world to come we would each have to account for any legitimate pleasures we denied ourselves in this world (J. Talmud Kiddushin IV end.).

This does not mean, however, that Judaism recommends hedonism; on the contrary, physical desire must be ruled by reason and regulated by law. In terms of bodily needs and functions, a union of physical and spiritual must be achieved. According to Maimonides, one must follow the dictates of nature in moderation; one must not be a

> glutton but will eat sufficiently to sustain his body with healthful food. . . . He will not be eager to stuff his stomach like those who gorge themselves with food and drink. He should not be so addicted to drink for "he who drinks to intoxication is a sinner and despicable, and he jeopardizes his wisdom" [as quoted in Weiss-Rosmarin 1965, 68].

This attitude toward the body ruled out the development of any type of asceticism within Judaism (with the exception of marginal short-lived movements such as the Essenes). The mortification of the flesh was seen as religiously unnecessary; Jewish piety does not consist in deprivation. For the Jew, abstinence goes against God's law since it is in essence a rejection of what God has created. It is a duty in Judaism to protect one's body; the preservation of health is a fundamental tenet of the faith. Maimonides wrote: "Since it is impossible to have any understanding and knowledge of the Creator when one is sick, it is man's duty to avoid whatever is injurious to the body and cultivate habits that promote health and vigor" (Hilchoth Deoth IV.1).

Our duty is not only to ourselves; each person must live as an active member of society. There can be no retreat from the world. Responsibilities to parents, family, and community are overriding concerns. Unlike Christianity, the Jewish faith does not have any institutions for those who withdraw from the general community. (Again the Essenes were a notable marginal exception to this overall pattern.) T. Weiss-Rosmarin explains:

> Jewish piety is not tested away from the turmoil of life but in the heart of its battle; sharing communal responsibility and rendering communal services are among its true marks for Judaism decrees: "Do not separate yourself from the community. . . ." The monastic hermit who withdraws from the world is therefore a sinner . . . he offends against the all

important commandment "Love your neighbor as yourself" [Weiss-Rosmarin 1965, 76].

This vision of human social responsibility is grounded in the belief that God made a covenant with the chosen people. Genesis portrayed God as the creator of the world who made a bond with the patriarchs; at Mt. Sinai God was revealed as the God of history: "I am the Lord your God, who brought you out of the land of Egypt, out of the house of bondage" (Ex 20:2). The prophets of Israel emphasized this theme, pointing out that God was the ruler of their national destiny. Thus the people must turn away from foreign gods and strange ways if they wish to prosper (Ex 20:5–6). Jews therefore see history not merely as a succession of events, but as the unfolding of an inscrutable divine plan. All that occurs is guided by God, and good will inevitably triumph. "I am the Lord; in its time I will hasten it" (Is 60:22). Nevertheless, God's action does not rule out human involvement. Israel is a partner in bringing about the fulfillment of God's promise for humankind. In this sense God's covenant with Israel is a covenant for all nations for, as Isaiah proclaimed, "I am the Lord . . . and have kept you; I have given you as a covenant to the people, a light to the nations" (Is 42:6).

6. THE TRUE ISRAEL

The hope of the Jewish people was not to bring the nations to Judaism, but to convert the whole world to God. They did not aim to establish a universal faith to which all believers must belong and in which salvation could be found. Instead they looked to the day when "The Lord will be one and his name one" (Zec 14:9). In the first centuries of the Christian era, Jews did attempt to proselytize, but eventually the rabbis came to see that there were other ways of spreading spiritual truth. Essentially they advocated dedication to a way of life that would inspire others. Adherence to the Law became a cornerstone of the faith. Ritual and moral prescriptions were scrupulously followed in the belief that such legalism did not interfere with Judaism's spiritual and ethical universalism.

Christianity however rejected this vision of the role of the Jewish people. Christians were, in the eyes of the church, the true Israel.

Paul declared that the Jewish people had been rejected by God (Gal 6:16). The Jewish faith was the religion of death (2 Cor 3:6). According to Paul the Jews were allegorically the descendants of Abraham by Hagar, whereas those who believed in Jesus were the descendants of Abraham by Sarah and thereby the recipients of the promised blessings (Gal 4:22–31). The Jewish nation had originally been God's chosen people, but when Israel failed to accept the Messiah, God declared the covenant null and void. The destruction of the Temple and the exile of the Jews from Israel were signs that Israel's mission had come to a close. According to Augustine, with the coming of Christ the Jewish people were "rooted out from their kingdom and were dispersed through the lands . . . and are thus by their own Scriptures, a testimony to us that we have not forged the prophecies about Christ" (in Silver 1956, 15).

The Jews thus became a living testimony for the church. They were not utterly destroyed, but were scattered throughout the world as a symbol of God's rejection of a people and the formation of a new covenant with the church. Indeed during the time of the Crusades it was argued by some Christian apologists that the Jews should neither be killed nor expelled because they were needed as a living symbol and witness to the truth of Christianity. Seeing their dispersion and persecution, Christians would understand the truth of the crucifixion and the calamities that overtook those who were responsible for it (Silver 1956, 16).

Under the old covenant the Jews offered their own imperfect righteousness in exchange for God's mercy and forgiveness; under the new covenant those without merit come before God in penitence. J. Atkinson wrote in *The Doctrines of Christian Theology*:

> All the hopes and ideals of the old covenant simply melt into the grandeur of such a conception of the new covenant. Here is the entire Gospel; here is perfect atonement. God is fully proved generous, and the new Israel is restored in a new relationship and under the new covenant of offering this gospel to the entire world [Atkinson 1969, 77].

This understanding of the new covenant rests on the Christian conviction that the Old Testament has been susperseded. Jesus is understood as the Messiah proclaimed by the prophets. Accordingly, the prophecy that Bethlehem would be the birthplace of the new King of Israel was utilized by Matthew:

> And assembling all the chief priests and scribes of the people, he inquired of them where the Christ was to be born. They told him, "In Bethlehem of Judea; for so it is written by the prophet: 'And you, O Bethlehem, in the land of Judah, are by no means least among the rulers of Judah; for from you shall come a ruler who will govern my people of Israel' " [Mt. 2:4-6].

In the gospels Jesus' messianic fulfillment was seen as foretold in the fifty-third chapter of Isaiah, where the tribulations of the suffering servant of God were described in detail. Such verses as the following have been interpreted as a compelling foretelling of the passion on the cross:

> He was despised and rejected by men,
> A man of sorrows, and acquainted with grief;
> And as one from whom men hide their faces
> he was despised and we esteemed him not.
> Surely he has borne our griefs and carried our sorrows;
> Yet we did esteem him stricken, smitten of God and
> afflicted.
> But he was wounded for our transgressions,
> He was bruised for our iniquities [Is 53:3-5].

Jesus' death seals God's covenant with the New Israel, and Paul justified this on the basis of Scripture. The divine promise to Abraham—"In thee shall all the families of the earth be blessed" (Gn 12:3)—referred to the followers of Jesus.

> So you see that it is men of faith who are the sons of Abraham. And the scripture, forseeing that God would justify the Gentiles by faith, preached the gospel beforehand to Abraham, saying, "In you shall all the nations be blessed" [Gal 3:7-8].

Jews, however, still rely on the old covenant with Abraham and look to the future for the coming of the Messiah. Their hope is the promise of God's future sovereignty over the world. The kingdom of God (*Malkuth Shaddai*) is a central theme of the Jewish liturgy. From ancient times the synagogue service has ended with the *Alenu* prayer, in which is expressed the hope that "we may speedily behold the glory of Thy might . . . when the world will be perfected under the Kingdom of the Almighty, and all the children of flesh will call upon Thy name." Judaism continues to rely on the traditional prophecies about the Messiah and looks to the time when all nations shall turn away from unrighteousness and be united in the belief in one God. Thus the kingdom of God is a this-worldly concept; it is about a spiritual development on earth.

7. THE KINGDOM OF GOD

This idea of a world kingdom arose initially out of the prophetic ideal of God's kingship in Israel. The more the monarchy came into conflict with the demands of the prophets for righteousness the greater did prophetic longing increase for the time when God alone would rule in sovereignty over the entire world. Then, as Isaiah proclaimed, "The earth shall be full of the knowledge of the Lord as the waters cover the sea" (Is 11:9). In former times God's reign was connected with Zion, from whose mountain God ruled as king. Later Zechariah declared that God is enthroned in heaven and God's dominion is over all the earth (Zec 14:9). The psalms too summoned all nations to acknowledge, adore, and extol God as ruler of the world. In the same vein Jeremiah proclaimed: "Who would not fear thee, O King of the nations?" (Jer 10:7).

Because their vision of God's kingdom was linked to belief in the coming of the Messiah, some Jewish thinkers interpreted this hope in nationalistic terms. Others dwelt on supernatural events. But in all cases the belief was that the kingdom of God would come to pass on the terrestrial level. According to Abraham Klausner the belief in the Messiah rests on

the prophetic hope for the end of this age, in which a strong redeemer, by his power and spirit, will bring complete redemption, political and spiritual, to the people of Israel, and along with this, earthly bliss and moral perfection to the entire human race [Klausner 1956, 9].

For Maimonides this kingly Messiah would restore the kingdom of David to its former state; the Messiah would rebuild the Temple, gather in the despised ones of Israel, and restore all the laws of the Torah that had been in abeyance (Yad. Melakim, 11:1).

The doctrine of the kingdom of God played a central role in Jesus' teaching: "And he went about all Galilee, . . . preaching the gospel of the kingdom" (Mt 4:23). He accompanied his teaching with miracles that were signs that the kingdom had come (Mt 12:28). He gave his apostles the mandate to preach the gospel of the kingdom (Mt 10:7). After his death the faithful were told that the suffering they endured would give them entrance into the kingdom (Acts 14:21–22). But in contrast to the Hebrew Scriptures, the kingdom in the New Testament was paradoxical in character. Contrary to the Jewish view that the kingdom of God would gloriously burst into history, Jesus preached that it would gradually unfold: It would grow like a seed (Mt 13:3–9, 18–23) through God's power (Mt 12:28); it would affect the world as leaven affects dough (Mt 13:33); it would gradually blossom into a huge tree that would house the birds of the air (Mt 13:31–32).

According to Jesus' teaching, the kingdom would develop through successive stages. It began with the mission of John the Baptist (Mt 11:12). Yet, as indicated by the parables of the mustard seed, the leaven, the weeds, and the fish net (Mt 13) there would be a period of delay between the inauguration of the kingdom and its fulfillment. This period covered the time between Jesus' entrance into the world and his return as judge; it was the time of the church. When this period ended the kingdom would appear in its fullness; the faithful would inherit the kingdom after a general resurrection and glorification of the faithful dead (1 Cor 15:50–55), when they would feast in the kingdom with the patriarchs (Lk 13:28).

For Jesus the kingdom was present but only in germ. Thus it was portrayed as an already existing realm, which must for the present tolerate the wicked existing side by side with the good. However, all would be remedied in the final eschatological fulfillment.

Throughout the gospels, Jesus was portrayed offering this promise. Reward in the final kingdom, he declared, would compensate for the ills of the present age: "Rejoice [at suffering] in that day, and leap for joy, for behold, your reward is great in heaven" (Lk 6:23). In the kingdom the righteous who had been resurrected would enjoy the heavenly banquet (Mt 8:11) with Christ (Mt 26:29). They would be as angels (Mt 22:30) and would shine like the sun (Mt 13:43). Thus the Christian vision of the kingdom is that it was already present in the ministry of Jesus although its culmination is still in the future.

Alongside the notion of the fulfillment of the kingdom in the future is the Christian idea of its fulfillment in another, spiritual world. In the fourth gospel Jesus declared: "My kingship is not of this world" (Jn 18:36). Out of this statement has grown the whole idea of an otherworldly heaven in a nonmaterial sphere. Thus within Christianity two ideas are in tension. One maintains that the fulfillment of the kingdom is in the future; the other that the kingdom is in a nontemporal dimension altogether. Both however are agreed that in some sense the kingdom has already arrived.

The belief in an already present kingdom has profound implications for Christian ethics. Jesus went far beyond the ethical teaching of the Jewish tradition. In essence his views on morality are an ethic of the kingdom of God since the germ of the kingdom has already arrived. In contrast to the legalism of Judaism, Jesus' teaching was an ethic of grace, and the moral demands that Jesus made are demands that arise out of God's initiative in establishing the kingdom. What was required for those who enter is not unquestioning obedience to the Torah but rather wholehearted trust in God, unlimited charity, and generous concern for others.

According to the gospels, Jesus did not undertake to give answers to ethical issues as did the Pharisees; he rejected the legalism of the Jewish tradition because of its emphasis on the letter rather than the spirit of the Law. According to the gospels, Jesus fulfilled the law by being faithful to its intention rather than to its precise wording. For this reason, he tended to illustrate the kind of action God requires by using parables rather than by citing specific ethical laws. This did not mean that Jesus was anxious to set aside the Law and the teachings of the prophets; he carried the law to its extreme conclusion by insisting that God's kingdom had arrived on earth and the only possible course of action was to live in complete harmony with its spirit of grace and love.

The central principle of Jesus' ethical teaching was a demand for total trust in God. Such dedication should, he believed, take precedence over all other commitments, including those to one's family, friends, or nation. In this connection Jesus emphasized that obedience to God embraces inward attitudes as well as outward acts; sinful tendencies must be rooted out. Nothing must come in the way of one's allegiance to God's rule. Further, Jesus declared that we must have concern for others. Even our enemies must be treated with loving care, since all human beings are potential citizens of the kingdom. In the Sermon on the Mount Jesus deliberately contrasted this attitude with one found in Judaism:

You have heard that it was said: "An eye for an eye and a tooth for a tooth." But I say to you, Do not resist one who is evil. But if any one strikes you on the right cheek, turn to him the other also. And if any one would sue you and take your coat, let him have your cloak as well. And if any one forces you to go one mile, go with him two miles. . . . You have heard that it was said "You shall love your neighbor and hate your enemies." But I say to you, Love your enemies and pray for those who persecute you [Mt 5:38–44].

8. SUMMARY

From this survey of the differences between Judaism and Christianity we can see that the understanding of Jesus as God Incarnate has had serious implications for Christian belief. Jesus is literally Son of God: he is the awaited Messiah. As God's anointed he ushers in the kingdom of God in which the Old Torah is superseded. Forgiveness, atonement, and salvation are offered through God's redemptive intervention in human history. Jesus summons all to enter into a new covenant with God based on divine love and grace.

This vision of messianic redemption, brought about by Jesus, is at odds with traditional Judaism. To the Jewish mind, God's covenant with the Jews is intact. The Messiah has not yet come. As has been the case throughout Jewish history, the Jews are still obligated to keep God's commandments. Their task for the present is to become God's copartners in maintaining and preserving righteousness, justice, and peace in an as yet unredeemed world. Because of these differences of understanding the two faiths have gone their separate ways throughout the centuries.

CHAPTER TWO

Jesus As Prophet

1. A NEW CHRISTOLOGY

Jesus has been understood through the ages as the risen Christ who sits at the right hand of the Father. The doctrines of the Incarnation and the Trinity have been central tenets of the Christian faith, and this perhaps more than anything else has made fruitful Jewish-Christian dialogue difficult if not impossible. As with traditional christology, liberation theologians also see Jesus as the Messiah, the Word made flesh, the Incarnate God. In the works of such writers as Leonardo Boff, Jon Sobrino, Gustavo Gutiérrez, Juan Luis Segundo, Ignacio Ellacuría, Jose Miranda—to mention only a few—this understanding is explicitly stated or implicitly assumed.[1]

Nevertheless, liberation theologians repeatedly emphasize that their concern is not to theorize abstractly about christological doctrines. Such traditional theological reflection, they believe, has been misguided. It has tended to obscure the figure of Jesus. Christ has often been reduced to sublime abstraction; this has led to a spiritual conception of the Son of God divorced from Jesus' concrete historicity. The practical consequences of such an attitude can be seen in the various charismatic sects that invoke the spirit of Christ but do not look to the concrete historical reality of Jesus for their inspiration (Sobrino 1978, xvi).

A theoretically abstract presentation of Christ has given rise to the view that Jesus was a pacifist who loved all human beings and died on behalf of all people in order to free them from sin. According to liberation theologians such an emphasis distorts the real nature of Jesus in that it exempts him from history and uses Christianity as a support for ideologies espousing peace and order (Sobrino 1978, xvi).

Liberation theologians further point out that if Christ is seen as the absolute in abstract terms, earthly matters tend to be neglected; in particular, the emphasis on the absoluteness of Christ can bring about an unquestioning acceptance of the social and political status quo (Sobrino 1978, xvii).

In light of these objections to traditional Christian speculation, liberation theologians insist that the historical Jesus should be the starting point for christological reflection. Gustavo Gutiérrez, for example, urges that Jesus be viewed historically:

> To approach the man Jesus of Nazareth, in whom God was made flesh, to penetrate not only in his teaching, but also in his life, what it is that gives his word an immediate, concrete context, is a task which more and more needs to be undertaken [Gutiérrez 1973, 226].

Following this impetus, Latin American Christianity stresses the Jesus of history over the Jesus of faith. In particular liberation theologians see a structural similarity between the situation of Jesus' time and the situation of the modern world. Oppression and persecution in contemporary society as in first-century Palestine, they believe, are contrary to the divine plan for humankind. In the gospels Jesus initiated a program of liberation; his struggle against the Jewish authorities illustrates the conflict that any project of liberation will provoke. The historical Jesus thus clarifies the chief elements of christological faith. By following his life and cause in one's own life, the truth of Jesus emerges. Leonardo Boff explains: "Jesus does not present himself as the explanation of reality; he presents himself as an urgent demand for the transformation of that reality" (Boff 1978, 279). By offering a critique of humanity and society, Jesus points the way to the fulfillment of the kingdom of God (Boff 1978, 280).

2. JESUS THE JEW

For Jews, liberation theology thus offers a new orientation to Jesus. As we have seen, in the past Jews and Christians have been unable to find common theological ground. Instead of attempting to build a bridge with Christianity, Jews have repudiated Christian claims about Jesus' divinity and Christians have denounced Jews for their unwillingness to accept Christ as their Savior. The doctrines of the Trinity and the Incarnation and the understanding of Jesus as the Messiah have separated the two traditions and have served as stumbling blocks to fruitful interfaith encounter.

Today, however, liberation theology offers a profoundly different direction to Christian thought. Unlike theologians of the past, liberation theologians are not concerned to analyze Jesus' dual nature as God and man; abstract speculation about the central issues of traditional christology (divine personhood, hypostatic union, etc.) have been set aside. Instead, liberation theology focuses on the historical Jesus as the starting point for Christian reflection. Jon Sobrino writes:

Our Christology will . . . avoid abstractionism and the attendant danger of manipulating the Christ event. The history of the Church shows, from its very beginning . . . that any focusing on the Christ of faith will jeopardize the very essence of the Christian faith if it neglects the historical Jesus [Sobrino 1978, 9].

What is of crucial significance for Jewish-Christian dialogue is the primary emphasis on understanding Jesus as a first-century Palestinian Jew. It is the flesh-and-blood Jesus of history who is of fundamental importance for liberation theologians; the concrete preaching and acting of Jesus provide the basis for the formulation of Christian theology. The historical context of the gospels is in this way reclaimed for Christians, and Jesus' teaching in the New Testament is related directly to God's design as recorded in the Old Testament. In particular, Jesus is viewed as following in the footsteps of the great prophets of ancient Israel. Ellacuría insists that prophecy in the Old Testament and Jesus' mission in the New Testament must be related.

> The prophecy of the Old Testament takes on its full ascendant import only in terms of what Jesus himself represents. By the same token the meaning of Jesus himself would escape us if we disregarded the history of prophecy [Ellacuría 1976, 23].

From a historical standpoint then the picture of Jesus that emerges from the gospel narratives is inextricably connected to his Jewish background. The consequence of this for Jews is profound for it opens the way to a fresh vision of Jesus' mission. His criticism of the religious establishment, like that of the pre-exilic prophets, should not be understood as a rejection of Judaism but as a call to the nation to return to the God of their ancestors. Seen in this manner, Jesus' teaching stands in the tradition of the ethical prophets of ancient Israel. We must turn to the prophetic books of the Bible to find the crucial links that relate Jesus to his Jewish past. In this context Jews can recognize Jesus as following the prophetic tradition even though they cannot say with the Christian liberation theologian that Jesus is "God of God, light of light, very God of very God, begotten not made, being of one substance with the Father."

3. THE PROPHETIC TRADITION

The earliest Hebrew prophet, whose book was dedicated to the proclamation of God's ethical requirements, was Amos, a shepherd from Tekoa who was active around 760 B.C. As in Jesus' day, then too the rich oppressed the poor, bribed judges in court, and cheated one another with false weights and measures. The religion of God, which had stressed the social justice of covenant law, had declined in importance and was thwarted by the king's syncretistic tendencies. In this atmosphere Amos railed against the people. Israel had sinned, he declared,

> because they sell the righteous for silver,
> and the needy for a pair of shoes—
> they that trample the head of the poor
> into the dust of the earth,
> and turn aside the way of the afflicted;

a man and his father go in to the same maiden,
so that my holy name is profaned;
they lay themselves down beside every altar
upon garments taken in pledge;
and in the house of their God they drink
the wine of those who have been fined [Am 2:6–8].

Amos reacted to what he saw: the rich exploited the poor;
women were used immorally; legal pledges were treated sacrile-
giously. Amos emphasized that observing ritual would do no good
as long as the Israelites continued to sin. Speaking in God's name,
he declared:

I hate, I despise your feasts,
and I take no delight in your solemn assemblies.
Even though you offer me your burnt offerings and cereal
offerings,
I will not accept them,
and the peace offerings of your fatted beasts
I will not look upon.
Take away from me the noise of your songs;
to the melody of your harps I will not listen.
But let justice roll down like waters,
and righteousness like an everflowing stream [Am 5:21–24].

Though some commentators have interpreted this passage as a
condemnation of every type of cultic practice, it is more likely that
Amos was here decreeing that cultic sacrifice by itself was not what
God required; it must be accompanied by a dedication to righteousness and justice.[2]

Amos continued his diatribe against unrighteousness by con-
demning luxury:

Woe to those who lie upon beds of ivory,
and stretch themselves upon their couches,
and eat lambs from the flock,
and calves from the midst of the stall;
who sing idle songs to the sound of the harp,
and like David invent for themselves instruments of music;
who drink wine in bowls
and anoint themselves with the finest oils [6:4–6].

In the midst of such self-indulgence, the rich remained unconcerned with the plight of the poor:

> Hear this word, you cows of Bashan,
> who are in the mountain of Samaria
> who oppress the poor, who crush the needy,
> who say to their husbands,
> "Bring, that we may drink!" [4:1–2].

Such indifference, he declared, condemned those who luxuriated in their wealth:

> O you who turn justice to wormwood,
> and cast down righteousness to the earth! . . .
> Therefore because you trample upon the poor
> and take from him exactions of wheat. . . .
> For I know how many are your transgressions,
> and how great are your sins—
> you who afflict the righteous, who take a bribe,
> and turn aside the needy in the gate [5:7, 11–12].

The merchants too were rebuked; they observed the holy days, but exploited the poor in the markets:

> Hear this, you who trample upon the needy,
> and bring the poor of the land to an end,
> saying, "When will the new moon be over,
> that we may sell grain?
> And the sabbath,
> that we may offer wheat for sale,
> that we may make the ephah small and the shekel great,
> and deal deceitfully with false balances,
> that we may buy the poor for silver
> and the needy for a pair of sandals,
> and sell the refuse of the wheat?" [8:4–6].

Several decades after Amos began his ministry in Israel, Isaiah began his prophetic mission in Judah. God had chosen Israel to produce justice, Isaiah proclaimed, but instead it created blood-shed (Is 5:7). Like Amos, Isaiah protested against the indifference of the rich to the poor and oppressed:

It is you who have devoured the vineyard,
the spoil of the poor is in your houses.
What do you mean by crushing my people,
by grinding the face of the poor? [3:14–15].

Isaiah condemned the offering of sacrifice without an accompanying quest for righteousness. Paralleling the message of Amos, he declared:

What to me is the multitude of your sacrifices?
says the Lord;
I have had enough of burnt offerings of rams
and the fat of fed beasts;
I do not delight in the blood of bulls,
or of lambs, or of he-goats.
When you come to appear before me,
who requires of you
this trampling of my courts?
Bring no more vain offerings;
incense is an abomination to me.
New moon and sabbath and the calling of assemblies—
I cannot endure iniquity and solemn assembly . . .
Wash yourselves; make yourselves clean;
remove the evil of your doings from before my eyes;
cease to do evil, learn to do good;
seek justice, correct oppression;
defend the fatherless, plead for the widow [1:11–13,16–17].

According to Isaiah, Israel was a sinful nation—a band of wrongdoers (1:4); the nation had turned away from God. Thus he condemned the women of Jerusalem who arrogantly and wantonly strolled through the streets (3:16–24), the priests and false prophets who drunkenly proclaimed their messages (28:7–13), and the judges who issued tyrannical judgments, cheated the poor, widows, and orphans, and grew wealthy on bribes (10:1–4).

The religious reforms of Hezekiah (715–687 B.C.) were over-turned by Manasseh (687–642 B.C.) who reinstated Assyrian astral deities and Canaanite fertility gods. This was subsequently attacked by Josiah's radical religious reform (640-609 B.C.). It is possible that Jeremiah was involved in this recommitment to covenant Law, to the destruction of the sanctuaries in the high places, and to the centralization of the cult in the Jerusalem Temple. Like Amos and Isaiah, he emphasized that God demands righteousness from the people. In a sermon delivered in about 609 B.C. he insisted that it was wrong to assume that Jerusalem was immune from attack because God's presence in the Temple provided protection:

> Do not trust in these deceptive words: 'This is the temple, of the Lord, the temple of the Lord, the temple of the Lord. . . .' Will you steal, murder, commit adultery, swear falsely, burn incense to Ba'al, and go after other gods that you have not known, and then come and stand before me in this house, which is called by my name, and say, 'We are delivered!' [Jer 7:4, 9–10].

Religious practice was of no avail if human justice and devotion to God were neglected.

The classical prophets, as well as the post-exilic prophets, who carried on and elaborated the message, became the conscience of the nation. They attacked the people's iniquity and the people's exploitation of the poor by the rich. God's covenant, they insisted, demanded compassion, justice, and righteousness (see Topel 1979).

For liberation theologians, Jesus belongs to this line of prophetic activity, which began with the eighth-century prophets and continued through the post-exilic period. Such a view of Jesus was grounded in the New Testament. According to the gospels, Jesus transcended prophecy, but was within the prophetic tradition. According to Ellacuría, the important thing to note here is that the people who lived with Jesus situated him in the prophetic line (Ellacuría 1976, 27). While their theological purposes might have differed greatly, the texts of Matthew 16:14 and Mark 8:27-33 clearly show that the people around Jesus placed him in the line of

Elijah, Jeremiah, and John the Baptist. In short, they saw him as one of the great prophets. It is in and through the prophetic dimension that the people and Jesus' disciples moved toward an understanding of who and what Jesus was in his ultimate reality. Hence one cannot grasp the ultimate reality of Jesus' life apart from his life as a prophet.

4. THE PROPHETIC JESUS

A central theme of prophecy in ancient Israel was the rejection of ritualistic and sacrificial acts devoid of an accompanying quest for righteousness and justice. The prophets were to be the social conscience of the nation.

> The Hebrew prophets' experience was of a God so concerned with human social justice and the demands he made on his chosen people that he was compelled to pour scalding words on his own people's infidelity to the law [Topel 1979, 49].

So too did Jesus see himself as the conscience of Israel in first-century Palestine. The ancient prophets condemned the leaders of the nation; Jesus attacked the Scribes and Pharisees for their iniquity.

Jesus believed that the Jewish leaders made a mockery of God's law. Thus he declared:

> Beware of the Scribes, who like to go about in long robes, and to have salutations in the market places and the best seats in the synagogues and the place of honor at feasts, who devour widows' houses and for a pretense make long prayers [Mk 12:38–40].

Like the Scribes, the Pharisees were also accused of betraying God's purposes. "For the sake of your truth," Jesus pronounced concerning them,

> you have made void the word of God. You hypocrites! Well did Isaiah prophesy of you, when he said:
> "This people honors me with their lips,
> but their heart is far from me;

in vain do they worship me,
teaching as doctrines the precepts of men" [Mt 15:6-9].

Again in true prophetic fashion Jesus reproached the Pharisees for their rejection of God's moral commandments: "But woe to you Pharisees! for you tithe mint and rue and every herb, and neglect justice and the love of God; these you ought to have done, without neglecting the others" (Lk 11:42).

We should understand Jesus' departure from Pharisaic law in this context. From the gospels it appears that Jesus was an observant Jew: he was circumcised, participated in Temple worship, attended the synagogue and observed the Passover. He rejected moribund, ritualized religious practices. For this reason he renounced the Pharisaic interpretation of scriptural law. Thus, for example, Jesus defended his disciples for plucking grain on the Sabbath (Mt 12:1-8). The Pharisees were unconcerned as to whether Jesus' disciples were hungry; their only interest was that the Sabbath Law not be violated. Jesus replied to their rebuke by trying to demonstrate the onesidedness of their interpretation. He reminded them that David transgressed the law that reserved the eating of the loaves of offering to priests. Furthermore, on the Sabbath the Temple priests performed their function without being accused of breaking the Sabbath. If they can do this, he argued, why cannot his disciples do the same in the new Temple, which is Jesus himself.

Jesus' aim was to show that his disciples' action could be defended by an appeal to biblical narrative and tradition. For Jesus, love must take precedence over law, even over the Sabbath. The error of the Pharisees was to believe that they were the only correct interpreters of the will of God.

They [the Pharisees] are the "just", those who know the will of God and faithfully observe it. Accordingly they can judge others. . . . But therein lies their deepest flaw. Their praxis is based on the law not on love [Croatto 1981, 50].

A second encounter between Jesus and the Pharisees occurred because of the presence of a paralytic in the synagogue on the Sabbath (Mt 12:9-14). Jesus was not dissuaded by the Pharisees' questioning and replied: "What man of you, if he has one sheep and it falls into a pit on the sabbath, will not lay hold of it and lift it out? Of how much more value is a man than a sheep!" (Mt 12:11–12).

Jesus emphasized in the next confrontation reported by Matthew that an act of compassion and love must take precedence over any legalistic prescription. Jesus healed a blind and dumb demoniac. When the Pharisees saw this, they said, "It is only by Beel'zebul, the prince of demons, that this man casts out demons" (Mt 12:24). In response Jesus pointed out that their conclusion was contradictory.

> Every kingdom divided against itself is laid waste, and no city or house divided against itself will stand; and if Satan casts out Satan, he is divided against himself; how then will his kingdom stand? [Mt 12:25–26].

Jesus' central concern here as elsewhere was to relieve human pain. Segundo remarks in connection with this passage: "The ultimate criterion in Jesus' theology is the remedy brought to some sort of human suffering, however temporary and provisional that remedy may be" (Segundo 1976, 79). The Pharisees, however, did not share this concern; they were, in Jesus' words, a "brood of vipers." "How can you speak good," he asks, "when you are evil?" (Mt 12:34).

In another passage in Matthew (Chap. 15) Jesus further emphasized the iniquity of the leaders of the people. Jesus was in Galilee when he was approached by the scribes and Pharisees from Jerusalem. "Why do your disciples transgress the tradition of the elders?" they inquired. "For they do not wash their hands when they eat." In his reply Jesus exposed them as transgressors of God's will and went on to explain that religious impurity is located in the moral, rather than the ritual, sphere.

> Not what goes into the mouth defiles a man, but what comes out of the mouth, this defiles a man. . . . Do you not see that whatever goes into the mouth passes into the stomach, and so passes on? But what comes out of the mouth proceeds from the heart, and this defiles a man. For out of the heart come

evil thoughts, murder, adultery, fornication, theft, false witness, slander. These are what defile a man; but to eat with
unwashed hands does not defile a man. [Mt 15:11, 17–20].

Mark records that Jesus explained, in relation to the healing on
the sabbath of a man with a withered hand, that it was justifiable to
violate the Law if good was promoted. The Pharisees watched
Jesus in the synagogue to see whether he would heal on the Sabbath
so that they could accuse him. Jesus said to the man, "Come here,"
and then he said to the Pharisees: "Is it lawful on the sabbath to do
good or do harm, to save life or to kill?" (Mk 3:1–15). To this
question the Pharisees had no answer, because, as Segundo explains,

faced with Jesus' question, they have no theological criterion
whatsoever and so they have nothing to say at all. Jesus'
question points up a level that is prior to any and all theological questions, a level where human beings make their most
critical and decisive options, i.e., the heart [Segundo 1976,
78].

Finally, a speech by Jesus recounted in Matthew, reminiscent of
the denunciations made by the prophets of Israel, summarized his
condemnation of the hypocrisy and iniquity of the leaders of the
people:

The scribes and Pharisees sit on Moses' seat; so practice and
observe whatever they tell you, but not what they do; for they
preach, but do not practice. They bind heavy burdens, hard
to bear, and lay them on men's shoulders; but they themselves
will not move them with their finger. . . .Woe to you scribes
and Pharisees, hypocrites! for you cleanse the outside of the
cup and of the plate, but inside they are full of extortion and
rapacity. . . . Woe to you, scribes and Pharisees, hypocrites!
for you are like whitewashed tombs, which outwardly appear
beautiful, but within they are full of dead men's bones and all
uncleanness [Mt 23:1–4, 25, 27].

Echoing the words of the prophets, Jesus also denounced the
iniquity of the rich. According to Ellacuría, Jesus put poverty into

a dialectical relationship with riches. "He condemns wealth," Ella-curía writes, "that makes people poor and produces poverty that points an accusing finger at the malignant reality of wealth" (Ella-curía 1976, 33). In the Sermon on the Plain (Lk 6), Jesus maintained that the poor will inherit the kingdom of God rather than the rich because they already possess the consolation of wealth. The hungry will be satiated while those who are now full will go hungry. Those who are now weeping will find consolation, whereas those who are happy will experience pain and tears. Further, Jesus asserted that those who have been persecuted for following the gospel will receive blessings as did the prophets of former times:

> Blessed are you poor, for yours is the kingdom of God.
> Blessed are you that hunger now, for you shall be satisfied.
> Blessed are you that weep now, for you shall laugh.
> Blessed are you when men hate you, and when they exclude you and revile you, and cast out your name as evil, on account of the Son of man! Rejoice in that day, and leap for joy, for behold, your reward is great in heaven; for so their fathers did to the prophets.
> But woe to you that are rich, for you have received your consolation.
> Woe to you that are full now, for you shall hunger.
> Woe to you that laugh now, for you shall mourn and weep.
> Woe to you, when all men speak well of you, for so their fathers did to the false prophets [Lk 6:20–26].

According to Jesus, the passion for riches was a major obstacle to the establishment of God's reign. Until the prophets appeared, material prosperity was understood as a blessing from God. But the prophets argued that wealth had reached the point where it resulted in the trampling and exploitation of the poor and oppressed. What was involved here was the recognition that wealth causes poverty. Therefore one was free to choose between being with the oppressors or being with the oppressed. For this reason, Jesus repeatedly stressed that God takes sides with the poor. Confronting the Pharisees, who were described in Luke as "lovers of money," he declared: "You are those who justify yourselves before men, but God knows your hearts; for what is exalted among men is an abomination in the sight of God"(Lk 16:14–15). In the same passage he stated: "No servant can serve two masters; but either he will hate the one and love the other, or he will be devoted to the one and despise the other. You cannot serve God and mammon (Lk 16:13).

The love of wealth makes it impossible for the Christian to establish a proper relationship with God. This point is emphasized in the account of the confrontation between Jesus and a young man seeking eternal life. Jesus first told the young man to keep God's commandments and he enumerated several. The young man however insisted that he already did this, yet he still felt a fundamental lack; he asked what must be done. "You lack one thing," Jesus admonished. "Go, sell what you have, and give to the poor, and you will have treasure in heaven" (Mk 10:21).[3] Hearing Jesus' response, the young man became sad and went off, and Jesus explained to his disciples: "How hard it will be for those who have riches to enter the kingdom of God" (Mk 10:23). He declared that it would be easier for a camel to pass through the eye of a needle than for a rich person to enter the kingdom (Mk 10:25).

It is the poor then who are to inherit eternal life; poverty is understood as a precondition for access to the kind of existence in which God is revealed. In the contest between poverty and wealth God takes the side of the poor. This unbridgeable divide between the rich and the poor is eloquently illustrated in Jesus' parable (Lk 16:19–26) about the rich man and Lazarus:

> There was a rich man, who was clothed in purple and fine linen and who feasted sumptuously every day. And at his gate lay a poor man named Lazarus, full of sores, who desired to be fed from what fell from the rich man's table; moreover the dogs came and licked his sores.

Eventually both died; the rich man went to Hades and the poor to Abraham's bosom. Pleading to Abraham for Lazarus to give him water, the rich man was told:"Between us and you a great chasm has been fixed, in order that those who would pass from here to you may not be able, and none may cross from there to us." Here God's predilection for the poor was spelled out and Jesus' words served as a warning to the rich who felt secure in their wealth.

Jesus' prophetic condemnation of hypocrisy, iniquity, and economic oppression was based on his conviction that the leaders of the nation had led the people away from God's true intention for them. He attacked those who claimed to hold the keys to the kingdom but refused entrance to others: "Woe to you lawyers!" he declared, "for you have taken away the key of knowledge; you did not enter yourselves, and you hindered those who were entering" (Lk 11:52). As the prophets had, Jesus challenged the false religion of Israel. In his ministry Jesus opposed a life of ritual observance devoid of a concern for righteousness and justice. In his preaching Jesus placed great stress on poverty over against wealth; for Jesus poverty was a precondition for God's revelation and salvation. These themes were present in Jesus' teaching from the beginning, when he quoted the words of Isaiah to indicate the nature of his task:

> The Spirit of the Lord is upon me,
> because he has anointed me to preach good news to the poor.
> He has sent me to proclaim release to the captives
> and recovery of sight to the blind,
> to set at liberty those who are oppressed [Lk 4:18].

5. JESUS' PROPHETIC MESSAGE

In placing himself in the line of the prophetic tradition, Jesus showed how anxious he was to call the people back to the true worship of God, and his words and actions testify to his dedication to compassion and loving-kindness. We have seen that Jesus healed the sick on the Sabbath in violation of Pharisaic law; in addition he conspicuously turned his attention to the lowly, to sinners, to children and to foreigners.

> All these persons suffer from a lack of something: health, life-prospects, prestige in the eyes of the "just," abilities, acceptance among Jews. They are all marginalized. And if they have any value, they cannot express it: the poor because nobody assists them or does them justice; the others because "religious society" punctiliously excluded the outcast: Jesus addresses himself to all the marginalized people, doubly op-

pressed by human egotism in general and by the "religious" structure in particular. He begins his liberation by giving value to their persons. They too are _human beings,_ but oppressed [Sobrino 1978, 50–51].

In the case of those who were most sorely in need, Jesus was able to illustrate the love and concern that we are all required to exhibit to our neighbors.

Jesus established fellowship with all those who were at the margin of society; he continually took the side of the weak who were ostracized and condemned by the general public. His approach was to accept all these people. For Jesus they stood within the pale of salvation; he conversed with prostitutes and welcomed outcasts; he ate with the dishonest tax collector Zaccheus; it is almost certain that he numbered freedom fighters among his disciples and women were among his closest associates. For befriending such individuals, Jesus was characterized as a "glutton and drunkard, a friend of tax collectors and sinners" (Mt 11:19). Nevertheless, Jesus asserted God's love for all humankind, even the wicked and ungrateful. It was these, he declared, who were sick and in need of a doctor: "Those who are well," he stated, "have no need of a physician, but those who are sick; I came not to call the righteous, but sinners" (Mk 2:17). As Luke recorded, Jesus came "to seek and save the lost" (Lk 19:10).

The response to this solidarity with outsiders was hostile: Jesus was insulted and defamed. He was called the companion of wicked people. He was accused of being a heretic, a madman, and a tool of the devil. Leonardo Boff explains:

It is through this sort of love and these mediating conditions that he senses the meaning of God's kingdom and liberation from the oppressive frameworks that create discrimination between human beings. One's neighbours are not just those who hold the same faith or belong to the same family or race; one's neighbours are all human beings [in Gibellini 1980, 111].

The figure of Jesus that emerged from these encounters was that of a man who gave himself to others, especially to those who suffered.

His was a love that united all peoples: "Whatever you wish that men would do to you," he declared, "do so to them; for this is the law and the prophets" (Mt 7:12). In the Sermon on the Mount Jesus emphasized in prophetic fashion that loving-kindness was the cardinal principle of human action, a total giving that demanded exertion, generosity, and responsibility. Such love, he contended, must extend even to one's enemies:

> You have heard that it was said, "An eye for an eye and
>   a tooth for a tooth."
> But I say to you, Do not resist one who is evil.
> But if any one strikes you on the right cheek, turn to
>   him the other also;
> And if any one would sue you and take your coat, let him
>   have your cloak as well;
> And if any one forces you to go one mile, go with him
>   two miles [Mt 5:38–41].

For Jesus, devotion to God necessarily entailed a selfless love for others. Thus when one of the scribes asked him which commandment was the most important, Jesus replied:

> The first is "Hear, O Israel: The Lord our God, the Lord is one; and you shall love the Lord your God with all your heart, and with all your soul, and with all your mind, and with all your strength." The second is this, "You shall love your neighbour as yourself" [Mk 12:29–31].

Salvation, Jesus contended, was decided on the basis of love for one's neighbor: When he was asked what must be done to attain eternal life, Jesus answered first by quoting the moral commandments (Mk 10:17–22). Such an orientation echoed the prophetic insistence on righteousness. By removing the emphasis on the legalistic and ritualistic dimensions of the Jewish tradition, Jesus illustrated that the love of God must necessarily keep one pointed in the direction of love for other human beings.

Jesus thus condemned all malevolent thoughts and actions. In the Sermon on the Mount, he decried hatred and anger:

You have heard that it was said to the men of old,
"You shall not kill, and whoever kills shall be liable to
judgment."
But I say to you that everyone who is angry with his brother
shall be liable to judgment [Mt 5:21–22].

Concerning lust he stated:

You have heard that it was said, "You shall not commit
adultery."
But I say to you that every one who looks at a woman
lustfully has already committed adultery with her in
his heart [Mt 5:27–28].

Jesus' words thus recalled the great prophets of ancient Israel,
and like them he utilized graphic images to emphasize the importance of love. We have already mentioned the parable about the
rich man and Lazarus; similarly Jesus explained in his parable
about the good Samaritan that love for one's neighbor must include
all people: neighborliness knows no boundaries of race or class (Lk
10:29–37).

In the life and ministry of Jesus then, we can see the bonds that
link him to his Jewish past. Like Amos, Isaiah, and Jeremiah, as
well as the post-exilic prophets who followed them, Jesus rebuked
the people for turning away from God. The Hebrew prophets'
experience was of a God so concerned with human social justice
that he was compelled to pour out his wrath on Israel for her
infidelity to the Torah. The prophets attacked the exploitation of
the poor by the rich because God demands not sacrifice but human
justice; they condemned the people for turning the worship of God
into a mechanical process divorced from the offering of a heart
committed to acts of loving-kindness. So too, Jesus condemned the
leaders of the people for their hardheartedness, hypocrisy, and
injustice. Love of God, Jesus insisted, must involve the love for all
peoples. By word and deed, Jesus attempted to convey the truth of
Isaiah's proclamation:

Is not this the fast that I choose: to loose the bonds of
wickedness, to undo the thongs of the yoke, to let the op-

pressed go free, and to break every yoke? Is it not to share your bread with the hungry, and bring the homeless poor into your house; when you see the naked, to cover him, and not to hide yourself from your own flesh? [Is 58:6–7].

6. SUMMARY

The vision of Jesus as a prophet of Israel calling the people back to true worship of God is at the heart of Christian liberation theology. Certainly for the liberation theologian, Jesus is more than a prophet. This prophetic understanding of Jesus should make it possible for the Jew to gain a sympathetic insight into Jesus' ministry. His attack on the scribes and Pharisees can be seen, not as a rejection of the Torah, but as a prophetic renunciation of a corrupt religious establishment. Such a conception of Jesus should enable both Jews and Christians to set aside previous christological barriers to interfaith dialogue and concentrate on a shared prophetic vision. Instead of rejecting Jesus as a blasphemous heretic, the emphasis of liberation theology can enable the Jew to see in Jesus' life a reflection of the prophetic ideals of Israel. In this fashion the Jesus of the New Testament can be understood as Jesus the Jew, who, like the great prophets of ancient Israel, struggled to rescue the nation from its iniquity and to draw the people back to the faith of their ancestors. The theologians of liberation present the Christian faith as being a further manifestation of the living tradition of social concern and idealism which has animated traditional Judaism through the centuries. Here then, in the life of Jesus as interpreted by liberation theologians, is a link that can draw Jews and Christians together in a mutual quest for the elimination of oppression and injustice in the modern world.

CHAPTER THREE

Ethics and the Kingdom of God

1. CHRISTOLOGY AND THE KINGDOM OF GOD

"My Kingdom is not of this world" (Jn 18:36). On the basis of this claim, traditional Christianity redefined the concept of the kingdom of God: the fervent Jewish expectation of a total transformation of the world was replaced by a spiritualized and individualistic hope for immortal, celestial life. The reign of God was no longer understood as a Jewish hope for the reordering of earthly life; rather it appeared as a heavenly promise that offered salvation for the individual. Within this framework, the temporal world was understood as having only preparatory value. The eternal realm by contrast was seen as the dimension of life in which the Christian could reach ultimate fulfillment and happiness. Given such an otherworldly outlook, Christian existence was significant only in that it could help the individual to achieve and express the religious and moral virtues that belonged to the Christian life. "The hope of the Kingdom, far from awakening an ethos to transform the world in the direction of that which was expected, worked as a deterrent for historical action" (Míguez Bonino 1975, 133).

In the history of the Christian transformation of the Jewish doctrine of the kingdom of God, Paul was the first and principal witness. For the Palestinians of the Jesus-movement, the crucifixion of their Messiah presented a deeply perplexing problem. But for Paul this event posed no difficulty; instead Jesus' death on the cross revealed the divine plan. "I have been crucified with Christ," he declared, "it is no longer I who live, but Christ who lives in me; and the life I now live in the flesh I live by faith in the Son of God, who loved me and gave himself for me" (Gal 2:20).

Paul's message was that God himself had entered through Christ into human sufferings. According to Paul, from the time of Adam sin had ruled over humankind: "Therefore as sin came into the world through one man and death through sin, so death spread to all men because all men sinned" (Rom 5:12). To save humanity from the bonds of sin God sent Christ to die in expiation. Pixley explains: "The cross in this preaching is the aim of Jesus' whole activity, and its centrality corresponds to the misery ('death') that is so characteristic of these masses to whom Paul preaches" (Pixley 1981, 91).

It was to the sinner then that Paul addressed his message. All have sinned and all are thereby liable to punishment. For this reason Jesus died to free humankind:

> While we were still weak, at the right time Christ died for the ungodly. Why, one will hardly die for the righteous man— though perhaps for a good man one will dare even to die. But God shows his love for us in that while we were yet sinners Christ died for us [Rom 5:6-8].

In this context Paul conceived of individuals entering the kingdom of God on their own rather than as part of a community. Under the influence of Pauline thought, the Christian faith was thus able to break with its Jewish origins and appeal to the masses as a spiritual religion unencumbered by feelings of national loyalty.

This conception of an internalized and spiritualized kingdom of God has worked throughout history as a deterrent for Christian action. Today however liberation theologians reject such an interpretation of the role of the church. Christianity, they maintain, embodies an ethic to transform the world; the gospel must galvanize the believer into action. Míguez Bonino writes:

> God builds his Kingdom from and within human history in its entirety; his action is a constant call and challenge to man. Man's response is realized in the concrete arena of history with its economic, political, ideological options. Faith is not a

different history but a dynamic, a motivation, and, in its eschatological horizon, a transforming invitation [Míguez Bonino 1975, 138].

For liberation theologians, historical events—economic, political and social—are intimately connected with the kingdom of God. "The elimination of misery and exploitation," writes Gutiérrez, "is a sign of the coming of the Kingdom" (Gutiérrez 1973, 167). Concern for the kingdom therefore involves a commitment to the future of humanity on earth. To seek the reign of God is to accept the duty of being involved in human history. Such a commitment "allows no basis for a spirituality of evasion which is uninterested in the problems of those among whom we live" (Davies 1976, 21).

2. THE KINGDOM OF GOD IN THE OLD TESTAMENT

God's kingdom is thus understood as intimately connected with the establishment of justice on earth. Liberation theologians emphasize that such a this-worldly conception of the kingdom is deeply rooted in the Old Testament. In the psalms, for example, God was extolled as a king who judges justly. It was he who righted injustice; he was the heavenly king who established and maintained justice on earth:

But the Lord sits enthroned for ever
He has established his throne for judgment;
he judges the world with righteousness;
he judges the peoples with equity.

The Lord is a stronghold for the oppressed,
a stronghold in times of trouble.
And those who know thy name put their trust in thee,
for thou, O Lord, hast not forsaken those who seek thee
[Ps 9:7–10].

This motif of God as the king who rights the wrongs of the world was related to the Israelite legal emphasis on the rights of the orphan, the widow, and the resident foreigner. Pixley explains:

Yahweh in his epiphany as the serenely enthroned sovereign is held responsible for the protection of the weak within his kingdom. According to the surprising Psalm 82 it is precisely this which makes him God, and it is because the other so-called gods do not right the wrongs of this world that they expose themselves as not gods [Pixley 1981, 17].

Psalm 82 reads:

God has taken his place in the divine council;
in the midst of the gods he holds judgment:
"How long will you judge unjustly
and show partiality to the wicked?
Give justice to the weak and the fatherless;
maintain the right of the afflicted and the destitute.
Rescue the weak and the needy;
deliver them from the hand of the wicked."

They have neither knowledge nor understanding,
they walk about in darkness;
all the foundations of the earth are shaken.
I say, "You are gods,
sons of the Most High, all of you;
nevertheless, you shall die like men,
and fall like any prince" [Ps 82:1–7].

God's nature was to be the divine king who acts justly, and Israel was enjoined to be like God. The Lord stood for righteousness and justice; so too must the earthly king act with loving-kindness and equity:

Give the king thy justice, O God,
and thy righteousness to the royal son!
May he judge thy people with righteousness
and thy poor with justice!

Let the mountains bear prosperity for the people,
and the hills, in righteousness!

May he defend the cause of the poor of the people,
give deliverance to the needy,
and crush the oppressor! [Ps 72:1–4].

Ordinary citizens too were called to the justice of God. By
keeping God's commandments Israel was to become truly God's
child by bringing peace to earth. When the people acted unjustly,
the psalmist called them to account:

Hear, O my people, and I will speak,
O Israel, I will testify against you.
I am God, your God. . . .

What right have you to recite my statutes,
or take my covenant on your lips?
For you hate discipline,
and you cast my words behind you.

If you see a thief, you are a friend of his;
and you keep company with adulterers.
You give your mouth free rein for evil,
and your tongue frames deceit.

You sit and speak against your brother;
you slander your own mother's son [Ps 50:7, 16–20].

Thus, as Topel explains, "the emphasis on justice, repudiation of
mouth-worship, and grounding of justice in the holy nature of
Yahweh indicate a theology of human conduct in every respect
congruent with the message of the prophets" (Topel 1979, 74).

3. JESUS AND THE KINGDOM OF GOD

Within this Old Testament context liberation theologians expli-
cate the meaning of the kingdom of God in the life and teaching of
Jesus. From the beginning of his ministry, Jesus preached that the
kingdom of God had come. After John the Baptist had been
arrested, Jesus announced: "The time is fulfilled, and the kingdom
of God is at hand; repent, and believe in the gospel" (Mk 1:14). For

Jesus the coming of the kingdom was a process that would culmi-
nate in a final eschatological climax at the end of time. This notion
was depicted in the parables of the seeds and weeds (Mt 13:24–43).
Then Jesus explained what was meant by the kingdom, which had
already become present in the life of his disciples:

> He who sows the good seed is the Son of man; the field is the
> world, and the good seed means the sons of the Kingdom; the
> weeds are the sons of the evil one, and the enemy who sowed
> them is the devil; the harvest is the close of the age, and the
> reapers are angels. Just as the weeds are gathered and burned
> with fire, so will it be at the close of the age. The Son of man
> will send his angels and they will gather out of his kingdom all
> causes of sin and all evildoers, and throw them into the
> furnace of fire; there men will weep and gnash their teeth.
> Then the righteous will shine like the sun in the Kingdom of
> their Father [Mt 13:37–43].

The kingdom of the Son of man would be made up of both the
good and the evil, but at the final judgment the good would be
accepted into the complete kingdom. The final kingdom therefore
was a future reality coming at the end of time; Jesus inaugurated
the first stage in this process of fulfillment. Topel explains:

> the kingdom of God announced and achieved by Jesus is like
> a mustard seed, planted in Jesus' own lifetime (Mark 4:1–34)
> and growing until the harvest at the end of time. Thus Jesus
> does bring in the kingdom in which people are freed for
> justice and peace, but only imperfectly, moving progressively
> to perfect justice only in the kingdom's final fullness [Topel
> 1979, 93–94].

Because he inaugurated the kingdom, Jesus had the power to
affect the elements of nature: "And he awoke and rebuked the
wind, and said to the sea, 'Peace! Be still!' and the wind ceased, and
there was a great calm" (Mk 4:39). Further, Jesus was able to
forgive sin: "When Jesus saw their faith, he said to the paralytic,
'My son, your sins are forgiven' " (Mk 2:5). Such an action "exem-

plified the same liberative activity of the Kingdom that is embodied in Jesus' other signs" (Sobrino 1978, 49).

In other passages Jesus revealed the meaning of the culmination of the kingdom. In the future kingdom, the time of the sinful would pass (Mt 19:28; Lk 17:26–30), sufferings would disappear (Mt 11:5), mourning would cease (Mk 2:19), death would be no more, (Lk 20:36), the dead would be resurrected (Lk 20:37). Furthermore, the old order would be overturned: Many that are first would be last and the last first (Mk 10:31), those who made themselves little would be great (Mt 18:4), the humble would be masters (Mt 5:5), and the oppressed would be freed (Lk 4:18). In addition, heavenly glory would be returned to human beings (Mk 12:25), the despised elect would be reunited (Mk 13:27), the children of God would meet in the father's house (Lk 15:23–24), and all hunger and thirst would be satiated amidst joyful laughter (Lk 6:21).

The end of the world thus began with Jesus' ministry; he ushered in the kingdom that is to be consummated in the Parousia. The breakthrough of the kingdom entailed a complete restructuring of the old order. This was the task that Jesus began. The announcement of the kingdom was therefore a call by Jesus to embark on the project of liberation.

> Jesus was only turning to the great prophetic line which required "mercy and not sacrifice," "contrite hearts and not holocausts.". . . For the prophets this demand was inseparable from the denunciation of social injustice and from the vigorous assertion that God is known only by doing justice [Gutiérrez 1973, 230].

Jesus could not help but denounce those features of social life that were inconsistent not only with the final kingdom but also with an anticipatory stage of it.

For Jesus the declaration of the coming of the kingdom was a call to struggle for the physical and spiritual liberation of the oppressed among whom he appeared.

> It is to such people that he addresses his proclamation of the coming Kingdom: to the sick, who are helpless in themselves,

and dominated by a stronger force; to the lepers who are cultically separated from the rest of society; to the Samaritan who is regarded as a schismatic; to the Roman centurion, who is foreigner [Sobrino 1978, 47].

Ellacuría makes a similar point in emphasizing that Jesus was a proclaimer and a doer of truth. "The import of this truth," he writes, "is liberty; it is a truth that sets human beings free" (Ellacuría 1976, 74). The figure of Jesus that emerges from the gospels is hence that of one who gives himself totally to others, especially those who are abandoned physically and morally.

By doing this he shows us that the established order cannot redeem fundamental human alienation. The world as it is cannot be the location of the Kingdom of God. . . . It must suffer a restructuring of its very foundation. . . . [For Jesus] it is love that saves, the disinterested acceptance of others and the complete opening of self to God [Boff 1978, 75–76].

In advocating such a radical transformation, Jesus criticized oppressive established institutions and groups that had enslaved the Jews. In Jesus' mind, the Temple was, as Jeremiah had previously decreed, a den of robbers (Jer 7:11) and not a house of prayer for the nations, which was its original purpose (Mk 11:17). So, too, did Jesus attack the Pharisees who were transmitters of the ideology of the cult that Jesus was criticizing (see Pixley 1981, 85). Jesus even extended his critique of social structures to include the family. The need to break family ties was demonstrated by the story of Jesus' own attitude to his mother and brothers:

And his mother and his brothers came; and standing outside they sent to him and called him. And a crowd was sitting about him; and they said to him, "Your mother and your brothers are outside, asking for you." And he replied, "Who are my mother and my brothers?" And looking around on those who sat about him, he said, "Here are my mother and my brothers! Whoever does the will of God is my brother, and sister, and mother" [Mk 3:31–35].

It is evident then that in the kingdom of God that Jesus envisioned liberation—from oppressive legalism, from suppressive institutional ties, and from convictions without foundation—was of paramount importance.

Such principles appear to have been put into practice by Jesus' followers. From Acts we know of the establishment of a community that put into effect the egalitarian practices that Jesus advocated.

> They practised a communism of consumption, sharing the goods that they had acquired by private means. (Acts 2, 44-45; 4: 34-35). Their leaders were James, the brother of Jesus, and Peter, one of the twelve chosen by Jesus as his closest circle [Pixley 1981, 86].

Jesus and his followers embraced within their communal life the egalitarian principles of God's kingdom that had previously been annunciated by the prophets of ancient Israel. Nevertheless, the disciples and followers of Jesus did not exhibit the full experience of God's justice and peace: these were simply stages in the dynamic and ongoing movement to a perfect kingdom, which is to occur at the end of time. The kingdom of God initiated by Jesus is like a mustard seed planted in Jesus' own lifetime (Mk 4:31-35), growing until the harvest at the end of time (Topel 1979, 94).

The kingdom, as understood by Jesus, was not a denial of history, but the elimination of corruptibility.

> God builds his Kingdom from and within human history and its entirety; his action is a constant call and challenge to man. Man's response is realized in the concrete arena of history with its economic, political and ideological options [Míguez Bonino 1975, 138].

The growth and ultimate fulfillment of the kingdom rests on a struggle against exploitation, alienation, oppression, and persecution. It embraces all: the world, society, and the individual. This totality is to be transformed through the activity that God has initiated but not yet completed.

4. CHRISTIANITY AND THE KINGDOM

Within this unfolding of God's eschatological scheme, liberation theologians maintain that Christians have a crucial role. It is the responsibility of each person to engage in the quest for the liberation of the oppressed. All Christians are obliged to offer assistance to this task not only in the religious and spiritual domain, but also in the spheres of politics, economics, and culture. "It is not enough to say that doing so is a condition for salvation; it is the very coming of the kingdom in its temporal form" (Bigo 1977, 131). The way of the kingdom implies the building of a just society. Gutiérrez notes that a situation of injustice is incompatible with the kingdom:

> The building of a just society has worth in terms of the Kingdom, or in more current phraseology, to participate in the process of liberation is already in a certain sense, a salvific work [Gutiérrez 1973, 72].

Entrance into the kingdom is open only to those who practice justice and distribute to the poor whatever they have over and above their own needs.

The heart of the gospel message is subversive; it embodies the Israelite hope in the end of the domination of some human beings over others. The struggle for the establishment of God's kingdom involves the overthrow of established powers: political involvement is imperative. To know God is to be concerned for the creation of a new order regulated by the principle of love.

> Our hope may refer to the Kingdom, to the second coming of Christ, but it begins here and now, in this society in which I happen to live and for whose transformation—humanization —I am inescapably responsible . . . loving one's neighbour, which is the first commandment by definition, today means working to change the structures that can destroy my neighbour, the people, the poor [Echegoyen 1971, 464ff.].

For liberation theologians such change involves the eradication of poverty, which is incompatible with a kingdom of love and justice.

Some theologians even go so far as to advocate the necessity of violent revolution as a means of altering the economic structures of society (Davies 1976).

The writings of these theologians express a common conviction that the rights of the poor must be upheld in a quest for the liberation of the oppressed. Peace, justice, love, and freedom are dominating motifs in their understanding of the coming of God's kingdom. Breaking with traditional Christian theology, liberation theologians emphasize that these are not internal attitudes; they are social realities, which need to be implemented in human history. Gutiérrez eloquently formulates this shift away from the values of the past:

A poorly understood spiritualization has often made us forget the human consequences of the eschatological promises and the power to transform unjust social structures which they imply. The elimination of misery and exploitation is a sign of the coming of the Kingdom [Gutiérrez 1973, 167].

Thus the kingdom of God, contrary to what many Christians believe, does not signify something that is outside this world. Each individual must make an effort to bring about a new order, a mission based on Jesus' actions and teachings as recorded in the gospels.

5. THE RABBIS AND THE KINGDOM

Of central importance for Christian-Jewish encounter is the liberationist's insistence that the coming of the kingdom involves individual participation in the creation of a new world. Though Judaism rejects the Christian claim that Jesus has ushered in the period of messianic redemption, Jews have steadfastly adhered to the belief that God is a supreme ruler who calls all peoples to join in bringing about the kingdom of God on earth. As we have seen, this understanding was an essential element of psalmist theology and a central theological motif of the Old Testament. In later rabbinic literature, this vision of the human role in bringing about God's kingdom was elaborated further. According to the rabbis, the kingdom of God would take place in this world; it would be established by human obedience to the divine will. The kingdom of

God consisted in a complete moral order on earth—the reign of trust, righteousness, and holiness among all nations. The fulfillment of this conception would ultimately rest with the coming of the Messiah; nevertheless, it was the duty of humanity to participate in the creation of a better world in anticipation of the messianic redemption. In the words of the rabbis, "Man is a co-worker with God in the work of creation" (Shab. 119b).

According to rabbinic theology, humanity is the center of creation for it is only human beings among all created beings who could through righteousness make the kingdom glorious (Agadoth Shir Hashirim, 18, 61). In rabbinic midrash, the view was expressed that God's kingship did not come into operation until human beings were created:

> When the Holy One, blessed be he, consulted the Torah as to the creation of the world, he answered, "Master of the world, if there be no host, over whom will the King reign, and if there be no peoples praising him, where is the glory of the King?" [Pirke Rabbi Eliezer, Ch. 3].

Only human beings then could make the kingdom glorious; God wanted to reign over free agents, who could act as God's partners in perfecting the world. But God required obedience to the ways of righteousness and justice:

> You are my lovers and friends. "You walk in my ways," God declared to Israel. "As the Omnipotent is merciful and gracious, long-suffering and abundant in goodness so be ye . . . feeding the hungry, giving drink to the thirsty, clothing the naked, ransoming the captives, and marrying the orphans" [Agadoth Shir Hashirim, 18, 61].

The idea of the kingdom was conceived by the rabbis as ethical in character.

> If, then, the Kingdom of God was thus originally intended to be in the midst of men and for men at large (as represented by Adam), if its first preachers were, like Abraham, ex-heathens, who addressed themselves to heathens, if, again, the essence of their preaching was righteousness and justice,

and if, lastly, the kingdom does not mean a hierarchy, but any form of government conducted on the principles of righteousness, holiness, justice, and charitableness, then we may safely maintain that the Kingdom of God, as taught by Judaism in one of its aspects, is universal in its aims [Schechter 1961, 93].

According to the Hebrew scriptures, God's identification with morality was absolute. In the prophetic writings, as we have seen, the primacy of ethical behavior was asserted, and this emphasis continued throughout rabbinic literature. Believing themselves to possess an authentic oral tradition as to the meaning of scripture, the rabbis expounded and amplified the ethical injunctions of the Bible. Thus throughout rabbinic literature, the rabbis sought to ensure that God's moral precepts were upheld. In this light the Jewish people were acceptable to God only when they fulfilled the commandments of the Torah. Hence we read in the midrash:

It is like a King who said to his wife, "Deck yourself with all your ornaments that you may be acceptable to me." So God says to Israel, "Be distinguished by the commandments that you may be acceptable to me." As it says, "Fair art thou, my beloved, when thou art acceptable to me" [Sifre Deut., Wa'ethanan, §36 fin., f75b.].

For the rabbis, morality and religion formed a single, inseparable whole. Faith in God entailed the obligation to be good, for God has commanded that the people follow the divine moral dictates. This view was eloquently illustrated in rabbinic lore:

It happened once that R. Reuben was in Tiberius on the Sabbath, and a philospher asked him: "Who is the most hateful man in the world?" He replied, "The man who denies his Creator." "How so?" said the philospher. R. Reuben answered, "Honour thy father and thy mother, thou shalt do no murder, thou shalt not commit adultery, thou shalt not steal, thou shalt not bear false witness against thy neighbour, thou shalt not covet." No man denies the derivative (i.e. the separate commandments) until he has previously denied the

Root (i.e. God), and no man sins unless he has denied Him who commanded him not to commit that sin [T. Shebu'ot III, 6].

6. JEWISH MORAL PRINCIPLES

Moral precepts are grounded in the will of God; in this light the Torah serves as the blueprint for moral action, and it is through the admonitions of the rabbis in Midrashic and Talmudic sources that the Jewish people are encouraged to put the teachings of the Law into effect in their everyday life. In the hierarchy of values, the rabbis declared that justice is of fundamental importance. R. Simeon b. Gamliel, for example, remarked: "Do not sneer at justice, for it is one of the three feet of the world, for the sages taught that the world stands on three things: justice, truth and peace" (Deut. R. Shofetim, V, 1 and 3). According to R. Elazar,

the whole Torah depends upon justice. Therefore God gave enactments about justice (Exod. 21:1) immediately after the Ten Commandments, because men transgress justice, and God punishes them, and He teaches the inhabitants of the world. Sodom was not overthrown till the men of Sodom neglected justice, and the men of Jerusalem were not banished till they disregarded justice (Ezek. 16:49; Isa. 1:23) [Ex. R., Mishpatim, 30, 19].

In explaining what was entailed in the principle of justice, the rabbis explained what was required in a court of law. With reference to the Deuteronomic injunction "thou shalt not take a bribe, for a bribe blinds the eyes of the wise" (Dt 16:19), R. Hama b. Osha'ya stated:

If a man suffers from his eyes, he pays much money to a doctor, but it is doubtful whether he will be healed or not. But he who takes a bribe, overturns justice, blinds his eyes, brings Israel into exile and hunger into the world [Tanh B., Shofetim, 15b fin.].

Regarding the statement "In righteousness shall thou judge thy neighbor" (Lv 19:15), the Sifra proclaimed:

You must not let one litigant speak as much as he wants, and then say to the other "shorten thy speech." You must not let one stand and the other sit [Sifra 89a].

Simeon b. Shetach said:

When you are judging, and there come before you two men, of whom one is rich and the other poor, do not say, "the poor man's words are to be believed, but not the rich man's." But just as you listen to the words of the poor man, listen to the words of the rich man, for it is said, "Ye shall not respect persons in judgement" (Deut. 1:17) [Ab. R. N. (vers. II), XX, 22a].

Like justice, charity was viewed as an essential virtue. The Talmud declared: "He who gives alms in secret is greater than Moses" (Bab. B. 9b). In another Talmudic passage R. Elazar stated:

Almsgiving is greater than all sacrifice for it says, "To give alms is more acceptable to God than sacrifices" (Prov. 21:3). But loving deeds are greater than almsgiving, as it says, "Sow in almsgiving, reap in love" (Hos. 10:12). Of his sowing, a man may eat or no; of his reaping, he will eat assuredly. And he said: "Almsgiving becomes increasingly perfect according to the amount of love that is shown in it"[Suk. 49b].

According to the midrash on the psalms, the gates of the Lord were open to one who cared for others:

In the future world, man will be asked, "What was your occupation?" If he replies, "I fed the hungry," then they reply, "This is the gate of the Lord; he who feeds the hungry, let him enter" (Ps 118:20). So with giving drink to the thirsty, clothing to the naked, with those who look after orphans, and with those, generally, who do deeds of loving kindness. All these are gates of the Lord, and those who do such deeds shall enter within them [Midr. Ps., 118:19].

Hospitality was also considered a cardinal virtue. In a commentary on Exodus we read:

God said to Moses, "I will send thee to Pharaoh." Moses answered, "Lord of the world, I cannot; for Jethro has received me, and opened his house door to me, so that I am as a son with him. If a man opens his house to his fellow, his guest owes his life to him. Jethro has received me, and has honourably entertained me; can I depart without his leave?" Hence it says, "Moses went and returned to Jethro his father-in-law" [Tanh, Shemot, §16,f87a].

Great is hospitality, the rabbi decreed, "greater even than early attendance at the House of Study or than the reception of the Shekhinah [God's presence]" (Sab. 127a).

7. THE NATURE OF JEWISH ETHICS

These few examples indicate that the kingdom of God is inconsistent with injustice and social misery; the effort to bring about the perfection of the world so that God will reign in majesty is a human responsibility. Jewish ethics as enshrined in the Bible and in rabbinic literature was inextricably related to the coming of God's kingdom. In this context a number of distinctive characteristics of Jewish morality are expressed in the Jewish tradition.[1]

First, as we have seen in connection with the prophets, there was an intensity of passion about the moral demands made upon human beings. For sins of personal greed, social inequity, and deceit, the prophet in God's name denounced the people and threatened horrific catastrophes. The voice of the prophet was continually charged with agony and agitation. Habbakuk, for example, declared:

Woe to him who heaps up what is not his own . . .
Woe to him who gets evil gain for his house . . .
For the stone will cry out from the wall,
And the beam from the woodwork respond.
Woe to him who builds a town with blood,
and founds a city on iniquity [Hab 2:6, 9, 11–12].

Such shrill denunciations of iniquity were the result of the prophetic conviction that people must be stirred from their spiritual slumber. "The prophet's word is a scream in the night . . . while the world is at ease and asleep, the prophet feels the blast from heaven" (Heschel 1955, 16).

Second, Jewish ethics requires that each person be treated equally. Biblical and rabbinic sources show a constant concern to eliminate arbitrary distinctions between individuals so as to establish a proper balance between competing claims. On the basis of the biblical view that everyone is created in the image of God, the Torah declared that false and irrelevant distinctions must not be introduced to disqualify human beings from the right to justice. The fatherhood and motherhood of God implied human solidarity; the Torah rejected the idea of different codes of morality for oneself and others, for the great and the humble, for rulers and ruled, for individuals and nations, for private and public citizens. Given this understanding of the equality of all people, the Torah singled out the underprivileged and the defenseless in society for consideration: "You shall not afflict any widow or fatherless child" (Ex 22:22). "Thou shalt not respect the person of the poor nor honour the person of the great" (Lv 19:15).

Since all of humanity is created in the image of God, Judaism maintains that there is no fundamental difference between Jew and non-Jew: God's ethical demands apply to all. In the Midrash we read:

> This is the gate of the Lord into which the righteous shall enter: not priest, Levites, or Israelites, but the righteous, though they be non-Jews [Sifra, Acharei mot, 13].

Indeed, according to the Talmud, the righteous non-Jew was accorded a place in the hereafter: "The pious of all nations have a share in the world to come" (Sanhedrin 105a). In this light, the rabbis emphasized that Jews must treat their non-Jewish neighbors with loving-kindness. One of the most authoritative rabbis of the last century declared:

> It is well known that the early as well as the later geonim wrote that we must abide by the law of the land and refrain from dealing unjustly with a non-Jew. . . . Therefore, my brethren, listen to my voice and live. Study in our Torah to

love the Almighty and love people regardless of faith or nationality. Follow justice and do righteousness with Jew and non-Jew alike. The people of my community know that I always caution them in my talks and warn them that there is absolutely no difference whether one does evil to a Jew or a non-Jew. It is a well-known fact that when people come to me to settle a dispute, I do not differentiate between Jew and non-Jew. For that is the law according to our our holy Torah [Spektor 1983, 134].

A third characteristic of Jewish morality is its emphasis on human motivation. The Jewish faith is not solely concerned with actions and their consequences; it also demands right intention. The rabbis explained: "The Merciful One requires the heart" (San. 106b). It is true that Judaism emphasizes the importance of moral action, but the Jewish faith also focuses attention on rightmindedness: inner experiences—motives, feelings, dispositions, and attitudes—are of supreme moral significance. For this reason the rabbis identified a group of negative commandments in the Torah involving thought. The following are representative examples:

> Thou shalt not take vengeance, nor bear any grudge against the children of thy people [Dt 15:7].

> There are six things which the Lord hateth . . . a heart that deviseth wicked thoughts [Pr 6:16,18].

> Beware that there be not a base thought in thy heart [Dt 15:9].

In the Mishnah the rabbis elaborated on this concern for the human heart:

> Rabbi Eliezer said, ". . . be not easily moved to anger" [Avot 2.15].

> Rabbi Joshua said, "The evil eye, the evil inclination, and hatred of his fellow creatures drives a man out of the world" [Avot 2.16].

Rabbi Levitas of Yavneh said, "Be exceedingly lowly of spirit" [Avot 2.16].

Connected with right thought is the Jewish emphasis on right speech. Jewish sources insist that individuals are morally responsible for the words they utter. Proverbs declared: "Death and life are in the power of the tongue" (18:21). Evil words spoken about one person by another could arouse hatred and enmity and destroy human relations. The rabbis considered slander to be a particular evil:

Whoever speaks slander is as though he denied the fundamental principle [existence of God]. The Holy One, blessed be He, says of such a person who speaks slander, "I and he cannot dwell together in the world" [Pe'ah 15d, Areakh in 15b].

There was also a positive aspect to this emphasis on human speech. Just as the rabbis condemned false utterances, they urged their disciples to offer cheerful greetings (Avot 1.15, 3.16, 12). Anger could be soothed with gentle words and reconciliation could be brought about (Spero 1983, 148).

A fourth dimension of Jewish morality concerns the traditional attitude toward animals. Since God's mercy and goodness extend to all creatures, "a righteous man regardeth the life of the beast" (Ps 145:9; Pr 12:10). According to Jewish tradition, human beings are morally obliged to refrain from inflicting pain on animals. The Pentateuch stipulated that assistance be given to animals in distress even on the Sabbath: "Thou shalt not see thy brother's ass or his ox fallen down by the way and hide thyself from them; thou shalt surely help him to lift them up again" (Dt 22:4). In rabbinic Judaism, this same theme was reflected in various midrashim. We read, for example, concerning Rabbi Judah Ha Nasi:

Rabbi Judah was sitting and studying the Torah in front of the Babylonian synagogue in Sepphoris, when a calf passed before him on its way to the slaughter and began to cry out as though pleading, "Save me!" Said he to it, "What can I do for you? For this you were created." As a punishment for his heartlessness, he suffered toothache for thirteen years. One day, a weasel ran past his daughter, who was about to kill it, when he said to her, "My daughter, let it be, for it is written, 'and His tender mercies are over all His works.' " Because the Rabbi prevented an act of cruelty, he was once again restored to health [Baba Metzia, 85a].

A final aspect of Jewish ethics is its concern for human dignity; Judaism puts a strong emphasis on the respect due to all individuals. This concept was found in various laws in the Pentateuch and was developed by the rabbis who cautioned that one must be careful not to humiliate or embarrass others. Maimonides, for example, wrote:

A man ought to be especially heedful of his behaviour towards widows and orphans, for their souls are exceedingly depressed and their spirits low, even if they are wealthy. How are we to conduct ourselves toward them? One must not speak to them otherwise than tenderly. One must show them unvarying courtesy; not hurt them physically with hard toil nor wound their feelings with harsh speech [Hilchot De'ot 6.10].

The Torah's concern for human dignity even included thieves. Rabbi Yochanan ben Zakai pointed out that according to the Law whoever stole a sheep should pay a fine of four times the value of the sheep; whoever stole an ox must pay five times its value. Those who stole sheep had to undergo the embarrassment of carrying the sheep off in their arms and the Torah compensated them for this indignity, but those who stole oxen were spared such embarrassment because they could simply lead the ox by its tether (Baba Kamma 99b).

8. SUMMARY

These specific qualities of Jewish ethics illustrate its humane orientation to all of God's creatures. Throughout biblical and rabbinic literature, Jews were encouraged to strive for the highest conception of life, in which the rule of truth, righteousness, and holiness would be established among humankind. Such a desire is the eternal hope of God's people—a longing for God's kingdom as expressed in the daily liturgy of the synagogue.

Here we can see the point of intersection between the Jewish faith and Christian liberation theology. For both Jews and liberation theologians the coming of the kingdom in which God's heavenly rule will be made manifest is a process in which all human beings have a role. The coming of the kingdom requires a struggle for the reign of justice and righteousness on earth. The kingdom is not—as it is in traditional Christianity—an internalized, spiritualized, otherworldly concept. Rather it involves human activity in a historical context.

Drawing on the Old and New Testaments, liberation theologians have attempted to demonstrate the tasks Christians must undertake in the building of the kingdom. Similarly, the rabbis elaborated the teaching of the Torah about human partnership with God in bringing about God's rule. For both faiths, the moral life is at the center of the unfolding of God's plan for humanity. Such a shared vision should serve to unite Jews and Christians in the joint undertaking of transforming our imperfect world in anticipation of the divine promise of the eschatological fulfillment at the end of time.

CHAPTER FOUR

Exodus and Freedom from Oppression

1. THE EXODUS FROM EGYPT

For liberation theologians Jesus is the liberator who paves the way for the realization of the kingdom of God on earth. In presenting this message of hope liberation theologians repeatedly emphasize the centrality of the Exodus from Egypt.

> The Exodus experience is paradigmatic. It remains vital and contemporary due to similar historical experiences which the People of God undergo. . . . It structures our faith in the gift of the Father's love. In Christ and through the Spirit, men are becoming one in the very heart of history [Gutiérrez 1973, 159].

Thus these Christian theologians look to the history of the Jewish people for inspiration in their struggle against exploitation and oppression in contemporary society, and this divine act of redemption of the Israelite nation provides a basis for a critique of traditional Christian thought and modern society.

In Egypt the ancient Israelites were exploited and oppressed. Elsa Tamez notes that this experience of oppression involved a degradation so severe that it caused the people to turn to God for deliverance (Tamez 1982). The Egyptians overwhelmed the Hebrew slaves with work; they "made their lives bitter with hard service, in mortar and brick, and in all kinds of work in the field; in all their work they made them serve with rigor" (Ex 1:14). Such affliction caused the people to cry out to God for liberation. In response God decreed:

> I have seen the affliction of my people who are in Egypt, and have heard their cry because of their taskmasters; I know their sufferings, and I have come down to deliver them out of the hand of the Egyptians [Ex 3:7-8].

Pharaoh rebuked Moses and Aaron when they demanded the freedom of the Israelite nation. "Why do you take the people away from their work?" he asked. "Get to your burdens" (Ex 5:4). Pharaoh's response to the people's request was to intensify their suffering. The same day

> Pharaoh commanded the taskmasters of the people and their foremen: "You shall no longer give the people straw to make bricks, as heretofore; let them go and gather straw for themselves. But the number of bricks which they made heretofore you shall lay upon them, you shall by no means lessen it" [Ex 5:6-8].

The intensified affliction however did not accomplish Pharaoh's aims, and to defuse the impending conflict he granted various concessions. The Israelites refused all his offers, and, as Elsa Tamez, notes

> the dialogue breaks off (10:28-29); the confrontation intensified and led finally to the liberation of the enslaved people. If the Hebrews had accepted Pharaoh's concessions, the struggle would not have become increasingly radical and the Hebrews would not have gained their freedom [Tamez 1982, 44].

In their exposition of the biblical account of the Exodus, liberation theologians underscore a theme that has become one of the central features of liberation theology: God is on the side of the oppressed.

> If there is a single passage that encapsulates the liberation themes of the Bible, it is the exodus story, describing God

who takes sides, intervening to free the poor and oppressed [Brown 1978, 88].

The Book of Exodus declared that God heard the groaning of the people and remembered the covenant with them (Ex 2:23-25). God took sides with the people, declaring that they would be liberated from their oppressors: Moses was to lead them out of bondage (Ex 3:7-10).

From this act of deliverance third-world Christians derive a message of hope: If God was on the side of the poor in ancient Israel, surely God still takes sides with the downtrodden. Thus if God has a bias today it is with the poor and oppressed. This means that God is against the Pharaohs of the modern world. Who are these Pharaohs? They are

the tiny minority at home who are in collusion against the great majority; they are the churches and churchpersons who give support to such oligarchies; and they are the rich and powerful from other nations who keep national oligarchies in power, thereby becoming complicit in the ongoing exploitation of the poor [Brown 1978, 89-90].

In the view of liberation theologians God works to liberate those who are oppressed by socioeconomic structures that are evil, exploitative, and unjust; those who seek to be coworkers with God in creating a just society must side with whatever forces are working for the liberation of humankind.

Liberation theologians stress that the exodus was not simply an event in the history of the Jewish people; instead it evokes a deep response on the part of the descendants of those who were liberated.

The word [Exodus] was "recharged" with fresh meanings by successive hermeneutical re-readings up to the time that it was fixed permanently as expressing a whole world-view in the Exodus account in its present form [Croatto 1981, 14].

The profundity of the Exodus therefore consists in its significance for later generations; the past holds a promise for those who understand its relevance. The Exodus is fraught with meaning. For third-world theologians it is an account of the liberation of oppressed peoples. They believe it is possible to understand the plight of those who are presently afflicted from the perspective of the biblical Exodus—the situation of peoples in economic, political, social, or cultural "bondage" (Croatto 1981, 15).

In this context liberation theologians stress Moses' crucial role in the process of liberation. Dussel, for example, begins his study of the history and theology of liberation by focusing on Moses' call to lead his people out of captivity (Dussel 1976). Moses fled to the desert because he had killed an Egyptian. He lived comfortably as a herdsmen with his wife, his father-in-law, and his flocks. But one day he heard God speak to him out of a bush. "Moses, Moses," God cried.

> I have seen the affliction of my people who are in Egypt, and have heard their cry because of their taskmasters; I know their sufferings, and I have come down to deliver them out of the hand of the Egyptians. . . . Come, I will send you to Pharaoh that you may bring forth my people, the sons of Israel, out of Egypt [Ex 3:7–10].

This divine encounter is represented by Dussel as follows (Dussell 1976, 3):

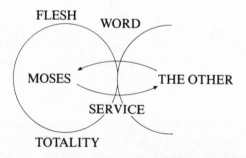

Here God—the Other—is revealed to Moses: Moses heard God's command: "Liberate my people out of Egypt." Established in the totality of fleshly, daily life, Moses responded by becoming the liberator of his people. We too are being called continually, Dussel contends, but we do not hear anything. Yet, like Moses, we must awaken ourselves to the divine command. "God . . . keeps on revealing himself to us as the Other who summons us. He is the first Other. If I do not listen to my fellowmen in bondage, then I am not listening to God either" (Dussel 1976, 7).

Liberation theologians also utilize the Exodus narrative to explain that God guides the destiny of the persecuted. In the flight from Egypt the Bible stressed that it was God who led the people. God did not take them out by way of the land of the Philistines although that was near, for God said, "Lest the people repent when they see war, and return to Egypt. But God led the people round by way of the wilderness towards the Red Sea" (Ex 13:17-18). When the Egyptian army attempted to capture the Israelites, God intervened and they were saved (Ex 14:24-28).

Once Israel had crossed the Red Sea, God sustained them in their wanderings: God gave them sweet water at Marah (Ex 15:22,25), sent them manna and quail in the desert (Ex 16:4-36), gave them safe passage through the Transjordan (Nm 21:21-24; Dt 2:26-37), and delivered the Amorite kings into the hands of the Israelites (Dt 3:12-17). Not only did God deliver and protect the people, God also led them to their own land where they were no longer oppressed. Before Moses' death, God proclaimed to Joshua: "I myself will be with you" (Dt 31:23). God promised to be with Joshua as God was with Moses (Jos 1:5).

The conquest was thus the second stage of God's deliverance, and even the prostitute of Jericho knew that God would take the side of the people as had happened in the past: "I know that the Lord has given you the land. . . . We have heard how the Lord dried up the water of the Red Sea before you when you came out of Egypt" (Jos 2:9-10).

According to some liberation theologians, a central element of the process of liberation is the use of violence. Paradoxically love and violence are interconnected:

> Love can be violent when the loved object cannot be retained or recovered except by force. . . . The history of the Exodus is eminently instructive in this respect. God acts with vigour. . . . "I will bring you out from under the burdens of the Egyptians" (Exod. 6:6); "I know that the king of Egypt

will not let you go unless compelled by a mighty hand"
(Exod. 3:10) [Croatto 1981, 29].

Here oppression is opposed by a liberating act that is violent—God
acted in this manner because there was no other option. At first
God sent Moses to try to persuade Pharaoh to release the Hebrews,
but Pharaoh's refusal left no alternative. As the upholder of justice
and freedom, God intervened to save the people; violence was
inevitably required.

> Justice is a radical good that demands of love (paradoxical as
> it may seem) a violent action. This is a truth so limpid that it
> shocks us because we have disfigured the image of love.
> Freedom, for its part, is a gift so intimate and exigent that,
> when it is obscured or lost, it requires liberation at any price
> [Croatto 1981, 31].

2. JESUS AS LIBERATOR

The Exodus is a pivotal event for liberation theology; it is regarded
as the salvation experience par excellence. To the Hebrew mind,
salvation involved a historical experience on the political and social
planes; God is viewed as Savior because God acted in human
history. In the unfolding of the divine plan of deliverance, God was
revealed through Moses, and, as Croatto notes, "Moses had to
assume that historical and personal vocation to freedom" (Croatto
198, 28).

Similarly, Jesus is viewed by liberation theologians as an emis-
sary of God; he is the typological correlate of Moses. The Exodus is
a central event in the life of the Jewish nation, and it serves as a
fundamental model of divine activity in liberation theology. The
departure from Egypt

> is much more than a mere image designed to enrich theologi-
> cal representations; it becomes the primeval and fundamental
> happening of the history of divine revelation itself. The
> Exodus comes to constitute the prototype of divine revela-
> tion, the privileged moment in which God once manifested
> himself and now continues to do the same [Fierro 1977, 141].

A number of liberation theologians connect the Eucharist with the struggle of the Jewish people for liberation. Like Moses, Jesus found his people oppressed and persecuted, and therefore he took on the task of liberation. He protested against injustice and iniquity; he sought to break down barriers between social classes and between Israel and the Gentiles. In carrying out his ministry he had to face great hostility, and it was then that he established the Eucharist (Balasuriya 1979). He realized that he would soon leave his followers, and he wanted them to have a symbol of his work. He used the Jewish Passover meal, giving it new meaning. Balasuriya states:

> To Jesus' mind the Eucharist was essentially action-oriented. It was a prayer and an offering in the midst of his public life at the height of his involvement in the political and social issues of the time. It signified his irrevocable contestation of the religious leaders of his people and the narrowness of their message [Balasuriya 1979, 17].

Confronting oppression in modern society, liberation theologians therefore rely on this category of Old Testament theology: Egypt is not a past civilization; it is a living symbol of oppression in the modern world. Sölle contends that Christians living in the first world have become contemporary Egyptians. "We have adjusted ourselves to the Egyptian lifestyle. We have adopted the basic beliefs of the Egyptians" (Sölle 1981c, 5).

Furthermore, we have tried to Egyptianize the whole world: "We see countries that have not yet adjusted to the capitalistic lifestyle and value system as 'not yet' developed" (Sölle, 1981c, 5). Yet, we in the first world fail to recognize that we are oppressors. On the contrary, Sölle advances, "we have adapted ourselves to it to such an extent that in the very midst of Egypt, under the domination of Pharaoh, we feel quite at home" (Sölle 1981a, 1). God as Emancipator can liberate us from our tyranny and lead us to a vision of a world freed from exploitation. "To remember Jerusalem in the midst of Egypt," Sölle writes, "means defining our need for liberation and denouncing the Egypt in which we live" (Sölle 1981a, 4). In the Exodus experience God has spoken to all humanity: In taking on the cause of the oppressed, God reveals the divine quest for the creation of a just society. The Exodus is the long march toward the promised land—a world free of misery and alienation.

3. THE EXODUS IN THE PASSOVER FESTIVAL

From this brief survey it is clear that the experience of the Exodus is typologically significant for liberation theologians; it is a paradigm of divine liberation of the oppressed and persecuted. Just as the Exodus is a key element in liberation theology so it has been a key to the self-understanding of the Jewish people throughout the centuries. In the biblical period, details of the Exodus were recorded in cultic sayings (Ps 107: 35–38), in Wisdom literature (Ws 19), and by the prophets (Is 63). After the exile the Exodus continued to play a dominant role in the Jewish faith. In particular, the festival of Passover was regarded as crucially important in the religious life of the people.

> The Passover celebration commemorates an event which will probably symbolize for all time the essential meaning of freedom, namely freedom devoted to a purpose. When Israel came forth from bondage, it was not simply to enjoy liberty, but to make of liberty an instrument of service. . . . The Israelites alone made the moment of their origin as a people one of permanent self-dedication to the principle of universal freedom as the essential prerequisite for spiritual growth. Hence the event has meaning for all living peoples [Finkelstein 1942, i].

The Passover Seder envisages the Exodus experience as a symbol of freedom from oppression, and the whole of the Haggadah is pervaded by the image of God as the Savior of humankind.[1] For this reason the Passover service begins with an ancient formulaic invitation to those who hunger or are in need to participate in the festival:

> This is the bread of affliction that our fathers ate in the Land of Egypt. All who hunger, let them come and eat: all who are

in need, let them come and celebrate the Passover. Now we are here—next year we shall be free men.

Any Jew who sits down to the Passover meal and is oblivious to the call of those who are in want has missed the meaning of the celebration.

During the service the leader displays the unleavened bread to stimulate the curiosity of the youngsters at the meal. It is then the turn of the youngest child to ask about the nature of the Passover festivities. The entire ritual of the Seder hinges on these inquiries. In reply the leader recites the narrative of the Exodus, stressing the themes of liberation and freedom from oppression:

> We were Pharaoh's henchmen in Egypt; and the Lord our God brought us out thereof with a mighty hand and an outstretched arm. Now, had not the Holy One brought out our fathers from Egypt, then we and our children and our children's children would be enslaved to Pharaoh in Egypt. Wherefore, even were we all wise men, all men of understanding, all advanced in years, all men with knowledge of the Torah, it would yet be our duty to recount the story of the coming forth from Egypt; and all who recount at length the story of the coming forth from Egypt are verily to be praised.

This response (based on Dt 6:21) implies that the Passover does not simply commemorate a triumph of remote antiquity. Rather the Passover ceremony is a celebration of the emancipation of each Jew in every generation, for had it not been for the Exodus Jews would still be slaves in Egypt. Historical continuity is at the heart of this understanding, and is illustrated further by the response made to the wicked son who asks "What mean ye by this service?" The leader responds:

> He infers "ye"; not himself. By shutting himself off from the general body, it is as though he denies the existence of God. Therefore thou shouldst distress him too, replying: "This is done because of that which the Lord did unto me when I came forth out of Egypt"—Unto me, not him; for if he had been there he would not have been delivered.

The keynote of the Haggadah is enshrined in a central pledge of the Seder:

> It is this Divine pledge that hath stood by our fathers and by us also. Not only one man hath risen against us to destroy us, but in every generation men have risen against us to destroy us: But the Holy One delivereth us always from their hand.

Here Pharaoh's action is seen as a paradigm of all attempts by Israel's enemies to persecute the Jewish people. Echoes of centuries of persecution are evoked by these words, yet it is made clear that God has been, and will continue to be on the side of oppressed people. In the symbols of the Passover meal, deliverance is reenacted. Explaining this symbolism the leader states with regard to the shankbone of the lamb:

> The Passover Lamb that our fathers used to eat when the Temple was still standing—that was because the Holy One, Blessed be He, passed over the house of our fathers in Egypt, as it is said: "Ye shall say, It is the sacrifice of the Lord's Passover, who passed over the houses of the children of Israel in Egypt, when He smote the Egyptians and delivered our houses." And the people bowed the head and worshipped.

The unleavened bread is the bread of affliction, the historical emblem of the Exodus. The leader declares that it is the symbol of sympathy for the enslaved as well as that of freedom from oppression:

> This unleavened bread that we eat—what is the reason? It is because there was no time for our ancestors' dough to become leavened, before the King, King of all Kings, the Holy One, revealed Himself to them and redeemed them, as it is said: "And they baked unleavened cakes of the dough which they brought forth out of Egypt, for it was not leavened: because they were thrust out of Egypt, and could not tarry, neither had they prepared for themselves any victual."

The bitter herbs, the symbol of bitterness and servitude, remind the Jews that it is their duty as descendants of slaves to lighten the stranger's burden:

> This bitter herb that we eat—what is its reason? It is because the Egyptians embittered the life of our ancestors in Egypt, as it is said: "And they made their lives bitter with hard bondage, in mortar and brick, and in all manner of service in the field, all their service, when they made them serve, was with rigour."

The lesson of the Passover service—deeply engraved on the hearts of the Jewish nation—is that persecution and divine deliverance are realities of the present as well as the past. In each generation, Jews must think of themselves as delivered from a perpetual enemy and should assume the responsibility of rescuing those who suffer under oppression. "In each and every generation," the Haggadah states,

> it is a man's duty to regard himself as though he went forth out of Egypt, as it is said, "And thou shalt tell thy son in that day saying, This is done because of that which the Lord did unto me when I came forth out of Egypt." Not our fathers only did the Holy One redeem, but us too He redeemed, as it is said, "And He brought us out from thence, that He might bring us in, to give us the Land which He swore unto our fathers."

4. THE PASSOVER IN RABBINIC LITERATURE

The Passover celebration is thus a symbolic exaltation of freedom; Jews are all to rejoice in God's liberation of their ancestors, in which each of them takes part. Throughout the history of the Jewish people this festival has awakened the spirit of the people to the significance of human liberation. The biblical account of the Exodus, embodied in the liturgy of the Haggadah, has played a central role in the Jewish quest for human dignity and freedom. When we turn to the Passover in post-biblical literature, we find that Jewish writers also saw in the Exodus a source of hope and inspiration, even during the darkest hours of Jewish history. The lessons of the Haggadah were taught repeatedly by Jewish sages in the Midrash and Talmud through commentary, interpretation, and legend; in this way new meanings were added to the biblical account.[2]

In Midrash Shemot Rabbah, for example, the rabbis explained why Moses was chosen to lead the Hebrews out of Egypt:

> Our rabbis said that when Moses our teacher, peace be upon him, was tending the flock of Jethro in the wilderness, a little kid escaped from him. He ran after it until it reached a shady place. When it reached the shady place, there appeared to view a pool of water and the kid stopped to drink. When Moses approached it, he said: "I did not know that you ran away because of thirst; you must be weary." So he placed the kid on his shoulder and walked away. Thereupon God said, "Because you have mercy in leading the flock of an animal, you will assuredly tend my flock Israel" [Midrash Shemot Rabbah 2.2].

In the Pirke de-Rabbi Eliezer, the rabbis emphasized the symbolic significance of the burning bush. Commenting on Exodus 3:2, they asked why God showed Moses a bush burning with fire. The reason, they maintained, was because Moses had thought to himself that the Egyptians might consume Israel; hence God showed him a fire that burnt but did not consume, saying to him, "Just as the thorn-bush is burning and is not consumed, so the Egyptians will not be able to destroy Israel" (Pirke de-Rabbi Eliezer, 40).

Similarly, when Moses asked God for a sign, the Lord told him to cast his staff to the ground, and it became a fiery serpent. This was done to illustrate that as the serpent bites and kills human beings, so Pharaoh and his people bit and slew the Israelites (Pirke de-Rabbi Eliezer, 40). Moses' hand became leprous in order to show that as the leper is unclean and causes uncleanliness, so Pharaoh and his people were unclean and they caused Israel to be unclean. Later however, Moses became clean again and God declared: "Likewise Israel shall become clean from the uncleanliness of the Egyptians" (Pirke de-Rabbi Eliezer, 40).

The rabbis emphasized that the God of the Israelites, unlike the gods of other nations, was the God of the living not the God of the dead. Thus, when Moses and Aaron stood before Pharaoh, they said to him: "We are the ambassadors of the Lord." When he heard their request, Pharoah became very angry and said: "Who is the Lord that I should hearken unto his voice to let Israel go? I know not the Lord, and moreover I will not let Israel go" (Ex 5:2). He then went into his palace chamber and scrutinized every nation and its gods. He then said to them, "I have searched for His name throughout my archives, but have not found him." Moses and Aaron then said to Pharaoh, "Idiot! Is it the way of the dead to be sought for among the living, or are the living among the dead? Our God is living, whereas those you mentioned are dead" (Midrash Shemot Rabbah 4.14).

The rabbis were anxious to point out that God was not responsible for Pharaoh's actions even though Scripture stated that God hardened Pharaoh's heart (Ex 10:1). Simon b. Lakish declared:

Let the mouths of the heretics be stopped up. . . . When God warns a man once, twice, and even a third time, and he still does not repent, then does God close his heart against repentance so that He should exact vengeance from him for his sins. Thus it was with the wicked Pharaoh. Since God sent five times to him and he took no notice, God then said, "You have stiffened your neck and hardened your heart; well, I will add to your uncleanness!" [Midrash Shemot Rabbah 13.3].

Yet, despite this action, the rabbis emphasized that God does not rejoice in the downfall of the wicked. R. Johanan asks: "What is the meaning of the verse, 'And one came not near the other all the night' (Ex 14:20)? The ministering angels wanted to chant their hymns, but the Holy One, blessed be He, said, 'The work of my hands is being drowned in the sea, and shall you chant hymns?' " (Megillah 10b).

5. THE PASSOVER IN LATER JUDAISM

Just as the rabbinic sources of the Tannaitic and Amoraic periods frequently alluded to the Exodus event as central in the life of the Jewish people, so too in Jewish literature of the medieval period were there frequent references to this act of deliverance. Judah Halevi explains why the liturgy stated that the prohibition of work on the Sabbath and on holy days was a remembrance of the departure from Egypt. These two things belonged together, he wrote, because they were the outcome of the absolute divine will. Quoting Deuteronomy 4:32–34, he asserted:

> For ask now of the days past . . . whether there hath been any such things as this great thing, or hath been heard like it? Did ever people hear the voice of God speaking out of the midst of the fire, as thou hast heard, and live? Or hath God assayed to go and take Him a nation from the midst of another nation, by trials, by signs, and by wonders, and by war, and by a mighty hand, and by an outstretched arm, and by great terrors, according to all that the Lord your God did for you in Egypt before thine eyes? [Halevi (1927) 1964, 114].

Saadia Gaon in *The Book of Doctrines and Beliefs* argued that the redemption from bondage was inevitable. God, he maintained, was just and would not do wrong. Having inflicted on the Jewish people prolonged suffering as a punishment, God set a time limit to their affliction. "Bid Jerusalem take heart and proclaim unto her that her time of service is accomplished, that her guilt is paid off, that she hath received of the Lord's hand double for all her sins" (Is 40:2).

Furthermore, God was a faithful keeper of promises; thus the promise that God would mete out judgment to the oppressors of the Jews and reward the Hebrew nation was certain to be fulfilled: "And also that nation whom they shall serve, will I judge; and afterwards, they shall come out with great substance" (Gn 15:14). For the trials of the past God would give the people a double of its double share—over and above what had been promised. Thus it was said: "And He will do thee good and multiply thee above thy fathers" (Dt 30:5). For this reason Saadia asserted:

> He mentions to us the Exodus from Egypt so frequently and in so many places. He wants us to remember the things we experienced. If anything which He did for us in the course of

the redemption from Egypt is not explicitly included in the promise of the final Redemption, it is implied in the statement, "As in the days of thy coming forth out of the land of Egypt, will I show unto him marvelous things" (Micah 7:15) [Gaon 1946, 168–169].

The Zohar, the medieval mystical book, relates that the joy of the Passover caused God to rejoice and call together all the heavenly hosts and say to them:

"Come ye and hearken unto the praises which my children bring unto me. Behold how they rejoice in redemption!" Then all the angels gathered together and observed Israel's singing because of God's redemption. Seeing this they also broke into rejoicing that God possessed such a people whose joy in the redemption was so great and powerful. For all that terrestrial rejoicing increased the power of the Lord and His hosts in the regions above, just as an earthly king gained strength from the praises of his subjects, the fame of his glory being thus spread throughout the world [Zohar, "Ray'a Mehamna," BO, 40b].

Modern Jewish writers of post-Enlightenment Judaism similarly emphasized the significance of the themes of liberty, redemption, and freedom as found in the Passover festival. Franz Rosenzweig, for example, argued that there was an intrinsic connection between the Passover and the Sabbath. The Sabbath, he maintained, is a reminder of the Exodus from Egypt:

The freedom of the man-servant and the maid-servant which it proclaims is conditioned by the deliverance of the people as a people from the servitude of Egypt. And in every command to respect the freedom of even the man-servant, of even the alien among the people, the law of God renews the awareness of the connection holding between the freedom within the people, a freedom decreed by God, and the freeing of the people from Egyptian servitude, a liberation enacted by God [Rosenzweig 1953, 319–321].

The Passover meal was a symbol of Israel's vocation as a people; the deliverance of the nation afforded a glimpse of its destiny. It was not only then that enemies rose up against the Jews; enemies have arisen in every generation, and God has always taken the side of the chosen people. All this pointed to the ultimate redemption as prophesied by Isaiah—of the day when the wolf would dwell with the lamb and the world would be as full of the knowledge of the Lord as the sea is of water (Rosenzweig 1953, 319–321).

The moral implications of the redemption from Egypt were emphasized by M. Lazarus in *The Ethics of Judaism.* The Exodus, he wrote, had a predominant place in the biblical and rabbinic cycle of religious ideas. The most exalted moral statutes in the Torah concerning the treatment of strangers were connected with the Exodus, and were, from a psychological point of view, impressively elucidated by means of the injunction: "Ye know the heart of the stranger" (Ex 23:9). The prophets and the psalmists used this event to illustrate God's providence and grace, and the rabbis deduced from it the two fundamental aspects of Jewish ethics: the notion of liberty and the ethical task of humankind. Throughout the history of Judaism, Lazarus remarked,

> the notion of liberty, inner moral and spiritual liberty, cherished as a pure, exalted ideal, possible only under and through the Law, was associated with the memory of the redemption from Egyptian slavery, and this memory in turn was connected with symbolic practices accompanying every act, pleasure, and celebration [Lazarus, 1900, 28–29, 231–232].

Kaufman Kohler saw in the Passover a symbol of thanksgiving and hope that sustained the Jewish nation in its tribulations:

> The Passover festival with its "night of divine watching" endowed the Jew ever anew with endurance during the dark night of medieval tyranny and with faith in "the Keeper of Israel who slumbereth not nor sleepeth" [Kohler 1918, 462].

Moreover, he believed that the feast of redemption promised a day of liberty to those who continued to struggle under oppression and exploitation:

The modern Jew is beginning to see in the reawakening of his religious and social life in Western lands the token of the future liberation of all mankind. The Passover feast brings him the clear and hopeful message of freedom for humanity from all bondage of today and of spirit [Kohler 1918, 462].

M. Joseph also focused on the contemporary significance of Passover (*Judaism as Creed and Life*). It is, he believed, the greatest of all the historical festivals in that it brings the Jews into close contact with the past. No other festival, he contended, so powerfully appeals to historical sympathies. At the Passover ceremony the Jews are at one with their redeemed ancestors; they share with the ancestors the consciousness of freedom, the sense of nationality that was beginning to stir in their hearts. "He [the Jew] shares," Joseph wrote, "their glowing hopes, the sweet joy of newly recovered manhood" (Joseph 1903, 213–215).

Through God's redemption the Israelites were able to free themselves from despair, and all Jews, past and present, share in this deliverance.

We march forth with them from the scenes of oppression in gladness and gratitude. The ideal of the rabbis fulfills itself. "In every generation it is for the Jew to think that he himself went forth from Egypt" (Pesahim 10:5) [Joseph 1903, 213–215].

Ahad Ha-Am concentrated on Moses the Liberator as an ideal type of hero. Moses, he pointed out, was neither a warrior nor a statesman. He was a prophet, who put justice into action. Confronted with acts of iniquity, he took the side of the victim. The events of his early life, when he struggled against injustice, served as a prelude to his revolt against Egyptian oppression:

That great moment dawned in the wilderness, far from the turmoil of life. The prophet's soul is weary of the endless struggle, and longs for peace and rest. He seeks the solitude of the shepherd's life, goes into the wilderness with his sheep, and reaches Horeb, the mountain of the Lord. But even here he finds no rest. He feels in his innermost being that he has not yet fulfilled his mission . . . . Suddenly the prophet hears the voice of the Lord—the voice he knows so well—calling to him from some forgotten corner of his innermost being: "I am the God of thy father. . . . I have surely seen the affliction of My people that are in Egypt. . . . Come now therefore, and I will send thee unto Pharaoh, that thou mayest bring forth My people the children of Israel out of Egypt" [Ahad Ha-Am 1946, 103–108].

In the modern period Jewish poets have also celebrated the message of liberation. Even in the Warsaw Ghetto, Passover had the power to move the hearts of those who endured suffering and death:

Pesach has come to the Ghetto again.
The wine has no grape, the matzah no grain,
But the people anew sing the wonders of old,
The flight from the Pharaohs, so often retold.
How ancient the story, how old the refrain!

The windows are shuttered. The doors are concealed.
The Seder goes on. And fiction and fact
Are confused into one. Which is myth? Which real?
"Come all who are hungry!" invites the Haggadah.
The helpless, the aged, lie starving in fear.
"Come all who are hungry!" and children sleep, famished.
"Come all who are hungry!" and tables are bare.

Pesach has come to the Ghetto again,
And shuffling shadows shift stealthily through,
Like convert-marranos in rack-ridden Spain
Seeking retreat with the God of the Jews.
But these are the shards, the shattered remains
Of the "sixty ten-thousands" whom Moses led out
Of their bondage . . . driven to ghettos again . . .
Where dying's permitted but protest is not.
From Holland, from Poland, from all Europe's soil,
Becrippled and beaten the remnant has come.
And there they sit weeping, plundered, despoiled,
And each fifty families has dwindled to one.

Pesach has come to the Ghetto again.
The lore-laden words of the Seder are said,
And the cup of the Prophet Elijah awaits,
But the Angel of Death has intruded, instead.
As always—the German snarls his commands.
As always—the words sharpened-up and precise.
As always—the fate of more Jews in his hands:
Who shall live, who shall die, this Passover night.
But no more will the Jews to the slaughter be led.
The truculent jibes of the Nazis are past.
And the lintels and doorposts tonight will be red
With the blood of free Jews who will fight to
    the last [Goodman 1961, 264–265].

6. SUMMARY

Reflecting on the significance of Passover, it becomes clear that Jews, like liberation theologians, have found renewed strength and hope in the message of the Exodus. The Passover ceremony unites the Jewish people with their ancestors who endured slavery and oppression in Egyptian bondage. Despite the persecution of centuries, the Jewish nation is confident of eventual deliverance and the ultimate redemption of humankind. The message of the Exodus calls the Jewish people to hold steadfast to their conviction that justice and freedom will prevail throughout the world.

Thus Jews and Christian liberationists share a common biblical heritage and vision of the transformation of society, and the Exodus event unites them in a common hope and aspiration for the triumph of justice. Remembering the divine deliverance of the ancient Israelites, they can work together for the emancipation of the enslaved. The biblical motif contains a reservoir of meaning for Christians and Jews alike in their struggle to create a better world. The Passover, by symbolizing the primal act of liberation, points to a future and ultimate redemption of the human family.

CHAPTER FIVE

Theology and Praxis

1. THE STRUGGLE FOR LIBERATION

We have seen that the Exodus is understood by liberation theologians as the central salvific event in the history of ancient Israel. The reign of Pharaoh was oppressive; in response God chose to create a nation of free human beings. The process of liberation began with violence. First Moses—upset by the cruelty of the Egyptian taskmasters—killed an Egyptian (Ex 2:12). Following this act of rebellion, a violent struggle ensued. The first-born of the Egyptians died (Ex 12:29-30), and God eventually prevailed when the waters drowned the Egyptian host.

Experiencing the redeeming power of their Lord, the Israelites burst into a song of thanksgiving celebrating God's defeat of their oppressors:

> I will sing to the Lord, for he has triumphed gloriously;
> the horse and his rider he has thrown into the sea.
> The Lord is my strength and my song,
> and he has become my salvation;
> this is my God, and I will praise him,
> my father's God, and I will exhalt him.
> The Lord is a man of war; the Lord is his name.
> Pharaoh's chariots and his host he cast into the sea;
> and his picked officers are sunk in the Red Sea.
> The floods cover them;

they went down into the depths like a stone.
Thy right hand, O Lord, glorious in power,
thy right hand, O Lord, shatters the enemy.
In the greatness of thy majesty thou overthrowest thy adver-
    saries;
thou sendest forth thy fury, it consumes them like stubble.
At the blast of thy nostrils the waters piled up,
the floods stood up in a heap;
the deeps congealed in the heart of the sea [Ex 15:1-8].

Liberation theologians emphasize that here love and violence are interrelated.

Love can be violent when the loved object cannot be returned or recovered except by force. Love for the other is "peace" when all is well, but it is "struggle" when injustice is present [Croatto 1981, 29].

Thus we read that God acts with vigor. "I know that the King of Egypt will not let you go unless compelled by a mighty hand" (Ex 3:19). If oppression is carried to the extreme of repression, liberation is necessarily violent. God acted violently in the Exodus account because the situation of the Hebrews admitted no other path. At first God sent Moses and Aaron to petition the king to allow their people to go. But the replies of Pharaoh illustrate that the oppressor never liberates. Therefore God turned to violence as a final resort. The demands of love called for a violent act. Why does God act in this way? It is because

oppression is never justifiable. Injustice can never be rationalized. Nor is it "tolerable" through resignation when legal or "peaceful" means to eradicate it are exhausted. Justice demands of love a violent reaction [Croatto 1981, 30].

2. HISTORY AND PRAXIS

The Bible is a record of divine intervention in human history. What was required of Israel was obedient participation in the fulfillment of God's plan of emancipation. The faith of Israel was portrayed as synonymous with acting in consonance with God's will. For liberation theologians the biblical witness leads to a historical orientation of the Christian faith. Praxis, rather than theological conceptualization, serves as the foundation of Christian commitment and obedience.

> Over against a theology of the word or of abstract principles, Latin America now posits a theology of lived faith, of committed action. Here a complete shift has taken place, and faith is understood as orthopraxis rather than as orthodoxy [Pérez-Esclarín 1978, 109].

For liberation theologians authentic theology must start from actions committed to the cause of liberation. In this service theology is a praxis of liberation. Within this context Míguez Bonino stresses that Christianity must concern itself with modern society.

> We are not concerned with establishing through deduction the consequences of conceptual truths but with analyzing a historical praxis which claims to be Christian. This critical analysis includes a number of operations which are totally unknown to classical theology. Historical praxis overflows beyond the area of the subjective and private. If we are dealing with acts and not merely with ideas, feelings, or intentions, we plunge immediately into the area of politics, understood now in its broad sense of public or social [Míguez Bonino 1975, 93]

Theology is here conceived as a critical reflection on praxis. In this context charity has been given a central place in the Christian life; it is understood as the motivating force, the giving of oneself to others. In this light, Gutiérrez remarks, "the understanding of the faith appears as the understanding not of the simple affirmation—almost memorization—of truths, but of a commitment, an overall attitude, a particular posture toward life" (Gutiérrez 1973, 7).

Similarly, Christian spirituality has undergone a major transformation. In the early centuries of the church, contemplative life was characterized by withdrawal from the world. Today, however, liberation theologians emphasize that religion must engage actively in modern life.

> The revitalisation of the religious life is come by way of our option for the poor classes on our continent. It is there that the following of Christ will find its embodiment in real history. If a people is capable of overcoming exploitation and building a fraternal society, in that very process it will be creating new forms of consecration to Christ and fidelity to our baptism [Cussianovich 1979, 164].

Christian action thus conceived must extend beyond the boundaries of the church. Instead of using revelation and tradition as starting points—as in the past—Christian reflection must begin with facts and questions derived from history and the world. As Gutiérrez notes, it is precisely this openness to the totality of human history that allows theology to fulfill its critical function vis-à-vis ecclesiastical praxis (Gutiérrez 1973, 12). Theology linked to praxis fulfills a prophetic function insofar as it interprets historical events in the light of God's purpose for humankind. The aim of such a theology is to make the Christian commitment clear and meaningful. Only in this fashion can the theologian engage in historical reality.

> He will be engaged where nations, social classes, people struggle to free themselves from domination and oppression by other nations, classes and people. In the last analysis, the true interpretation of the meaning revealed by theology is achieved only in historical praxis [Gutiérrez 1973, 13].

Liberation theologians insist that theology and action are inextricably linked. In the past many theologians believed that timeless truths could be applied to a finished universe. In contrast to this traditional view, both the world and human comprehension are viewed as incomplete; each requires refinement and development. Gutiérrez said that "knowledge is not the conformity of the mind to the given, but an immersion in the process of transformation and construction of a new world" (in Brown 1978, 71). This process involves a constant interaction of practice and theory. For the

Christian, praxis is a means by which a new heaven and a new earth can be formed. It is transforming action in tension with theory. Praxis therefore grows out of and responds to historical circumstance. Further, it is subversive engagement:

> Since it is praxis committed to the poor and to the transformation of the world, undertaken from "the view below," we can describe it, in the precise technical meaning of the word, as subversive action [Brown 1978, 72].

Thus theology is a critical reflection on historical activity. Unlike traditional theology, which was concerned with eternal realities, liberation theology is oriented to action. Truth is not defined a priori, independent of its historical verification; the theology of liberation insists on a historical basis. Faith can only be historically true when it becomes true, when it is effective in the liberation of humankind. In this way the truth dimension of faith is directly linked to its ethical and political dimensions (Assmann 1975, 81).

Such a historically rooted view of theology has serious implications for understanding the meaning of Jesus' ministry. A theology of the cross must be stripped of alienating mystifications. Instead of seeing Jesus as the scapegoat and reconciler, the theology of liberation aims to give back to the man Jesus his full integrity as a human being and to give his death its real historical and political meaning. From this vantage point, liberationists argue, it is possible to unravel the true meaning behind the symbolism of the passion narrative (Assman 1975, 86).

3. THEOLOGY AND MARXISM

In rendering an account of historical reality, liberation theologians have appealed to the social sciences to provide a basis for their view of society. In the past Christians utilized various philosophical systems to elaborate their views of God and humanity; for this reason liberationists feel fully justified in appropriating certain features of Marxist thought. Marxism, they believe, is an instrument of social analysis. By using the Marxist framework, liberation theologians find themselves better able to understand the world.

The interpretive context reveals that society is in a state of conflict in which major forces are polarized, unable to work together: the oppressors and the oppressed. Those who are exploited are not in control of their destiny; they are economically, politically, and culturally dependent on others. Class struggle is thus a fact of life; to deny its reality is to side with the oppressors.

When the Church rejects the class struggle, it is objectively operating as a part of the prevailing system. By denying the existence of social division, this system seeks to perpetuate this division on which are based the privileges of its beneficiaries [Gutiérrez 1973, 275].

In such situations, one must inevitably take sides. Not to do so is in fact a decision to side with those in power; neutrality is impossible. In the past Christians tended to interpret evil in individualistic terms. Liberation theologians however insist that a society must itself change if evil is to be eliminated. For this reason, social and political action are central to the church's message.

A Marxist perspective provides a basis for understanding the nature of class conflict. For liberation theologians the struggle against oppression is seen as necessary and critical. The outcome of this conflict is not a new oppression, but the suppression of oppression and the elimination of evil. Míguez Bonino explains:

Class struggle is not seen as a permanent fate of human existence and history but as an evil, triggered by the oppressive character of the present economic (social and political) system; an evil that we must try to overcome by the elimination of this system [Míguez Bonino 1975, 107].

The quest for a more human understanding of work is linked to class struggle. According to Marxism, workers in capitalist society are estranged from their work; labor is simply a purchased commodity. The response of many Christian liberation theologians is to protest against this dehumanized conception of human toil. What is needed instead is for laborers to realize themselves in their work. This can only be done, liberationists insist, by changing the structure of production, by replacing capitalism with socialism.

Socialism, which is characterized by social appropriation of the means of production, paves the way for a new economy which makes possible autonomous development at a more accelerated pace and which ovecomes the division of society into antagonistic classes. But socialism is not just a new economy. It should also generate new values which will pave the way for a society that evinces more fellowship and brotherhood. In this society the worker will shoulder his proper role with new dignity [Eagleson 1975, 3].

Such a structure, liberationists believe, will provide a basis for recovering the real meaning of work and reestablish a proper relationship between laborers and the products they create.

According to some liberation theologians, such a transformation of society can only take place through violent revolution. The theory of revolution is based on an analysis of the structures of injustice and oppression. Inevitably those who possess wealth and power will resist change. "So we are presented," Ellacuría writes, "with the necessity of exerting force against the unjust will of those who hold power in the oppressive structural setup which crucifies the weak" (Ellacuría 1976, 209).

Violence is therefore legitimate if it is used to redeem the enslaved. In this context the struggle against violence should not be regarded as violence; instead it should be seen as a force that is necessary to redeem the established violence against humankind. Such an understanding is well illustrated in the life of Camilo Torres, the Colombian priest who died as a guerrilla fighter. He believed that taking part in the revolutionary struggle was a Christian and priestly act. Love could, he felt, only be sustained through revolution, and he therefore established a political faction. Eventually he joined the guerrillas and was killed in a military encounter.

Camilo Torres represents an extreme position within liberation theology; nevertheless liberationists agree that social and political action is necessary in the face of exploitation, oppression, and injustice. In attempting to liberate humankind from servitude, liberation theologians have been guided by the vision of a utopian society. Their quest involves the creation of a new social consciousness and political structure. To accomplish this objective, faith and action must go hand in hand.

Faith and political action will not enter into a correct and fruitful relationship except through the effort to create a new type of person in a different society. . . . Political liberation appears as a path toward the utopia of a freer, more human man, the protagonist of his own history [Gutiérrez 1973, 236].

Such a conception of utopia proclaims that human unity is possible through the abolition of human exploitation. In the view of liberation theologians, God calls us to the task of humanizing social and economic structures. Belief in God places humankind at the heart of the historical struggle for justice and freedom proclaimed by both the prophets of the Old Testament and Jesus in the gospels.

The belief in a utopian vision of the future to be created through human action is far removed from traditional Christian eschatology. As we have seen, the hope of the kingdom worked against social and political activity; liberation theologians aim to change the world, and their writings are intended to galvanize others into action. In transforming Christian thought, these Christian writers look to their Jewish heritage for models of divine activity. In the Exodus narrative in particular they find the essential elements of a theology in which divine will and human response were bound together. Thus the Jewish scriptures serve as the starting point for a theology of liberation in which

God's action takes place in history and as history. It inextricably involves human action and, conversely, there is no human action reported outside the relation with God's purpose and world. . . . Yahweh's sovereignty does not appear in history as an abstract act or an interpretation but as announcement and commandment, as an announcement which convokes, as promise and judgment demanding and inviting a response [Míguez Bonino 1975, 134].

4. JUDAISM AND MORAL ACTION

Here then we can see the Jewish background to this emphasis on the significance of history in liberation theology. For Jews, as for liberationists, history matters. The Jewish hope for the future lies in God's sovereign rule on earth. From ancient times the synagogue liturgy concluded with a prayer in which this hope was expressed:

> May we speedily behold the glory of Thy might,
> when Thou wilt remove the abominations from the earth,
> and the idols will be utterly cut off;
> when the world will be perfected under the kingdom of the
>   Almighty,
> and all the children of flesh will call upon Thy name;
> when Thou wilt turn unto Thyself all the wicked of the earth.

This is the goal of the history of the world in which God's chosen people have a central role. In this context the people of Israel have a historical mission to be a light to the nations. Through Moses God addressed the people and declared:

> You have seen what I did to the Egyptians, and how I bore you on eagles' wings, and brought you unto myself. Now therefore, if you will obey my voice and keep my covenant, you shall be my own possession among all peoples; for all the earth is mine, and you shall be to me a kingdom of priests and a holy nation [Ex 19:4–6].

Election was to be a servant of the Lord, to proclaim God's truth and righteousness throughout the world. Being chosen meant duty and responsibility; it was

> a divine call persisting through all ages and encompassing all lands, a continuous activity of the spirit which has ever summoned for itself new heralds and heroes to testify to truth, justice and sublime faith [Kohler (1918) 1968, 326].

Judaism did not separate religion from life; instead Jews were called to action, to turn humankind away from violence, wickedness, and falsehood. It was not the hope of bliss in a future life but the establishment of the kingdom of justice and peace that was central to the Jewish faith. Moral praxis was at the heart of the religious tradition. The people of Israel as a light to the nations reflected the moral nature of God; each Jew was to be like the creator, mirroring the divine qualities revealed to Moses: "The Lord, the Lord, a God merciful and gracious, slow to anger, and abounding in steadfast love and faithfulness, keeping steadfast love for thousands, forgiving iniquity and transgression and sin" (Ex 34:6-7).

God as a moral being demanded moral living, as the Psalms declared: "The Lord is righteous; He loves righteous deeds" (Ps 11:7). "Righteousness and justice are the foundation of His throne" (Ps 97:2). "Thou hast established equity; thou hast executed justice and righteousness" (Ps 99:4). Given this theological framework, Jews were directed to obey the revealed will of God, which was the basis of the covenantal relationship between God and the Jewish nation. Orthopraxis, rather than conceptual reflection, served as the foundation of the religion of Israel.

In the Bible, deeds and events involving moral issues could be found in abundance: the punishment of Cain for murdering his brother, the violence of the generation that brought on the flood, the early prohibition against murder, the hospitality of Abraham and his pleading for the people of Sodom, the praise of Abraham for his moral attitudes, the condemnation of Joseph's brothers, Joseph's self-restraint in the house of Potiphar, Moses' intercessions on the side of the exploited (Spero 1983, 22).

But it is preeminently in the legal codes of the Pentateuch that we encounter moral guidelines formulated in specific rules. The Decalogue in particular illustrates the centrality of moral praxis in the life of the Jew. The first four commandments are theological in character, but the last six deal with relationships between human beings. The first commandment describes God as the one who redeemed the Jews from Egypt; the one who forbade the worship of other deities and demanded respect for the Sabbath and the divine name. These commandments were expressions of the love and fear of God; the remaining injunctions provided a means of expressing love of other human beings. The Decalogue made it clear that moral rules were fundamental to the Jewish faith.

Such ethical standards were repeated in the prophetic books. The teachings of the prophets were rooted in the Torah of Moses. The prophets saw themselves as messengers of the divine word; their special task was to denounce the people for their transgressions and call them to repentance. In all this they pointed to concrete action—moral praxis—as the only means of sustaining the covenantal relationship with God. The essential theme of their message was that God demanded righteousness and justice.

Emphasis on the moral life was reflected in the prophetic condemnation of cultic practices that were not accompanied by ethical concern. These passages illustrated that ritual commandments were of instrumental value; morality was intrinisic and absolute. The primacy of morality was also reflected in the prophetic warning that righteous action was the determining factor in the destiny of the Jewish nation. Moral transgressions referred to in such contexts concerned exploitation, oppression, and the perversion of justice. These sins had the potential to bring about the downfall of the nation.

The Book of Proverbs reinforced the teaching of the Torah and the prophets; wisdom was conceived here as a capacity to act morally; it was a skill that could be learned. Throughout Proverbs dispositional traits were catalogued: the positive moral types included the *tzaddik*, the *chakham*, and the *yashar*, the evil characters included the *rasha*, the *avil*, the *kheseil*, the *letz*, and the *peti*.

> This suggests that moral virtue or vice is to be achieved not by concentrating on individual moral acts but rather by learning to recognise and emulate certain good personality types [Spero 1983, 42].

Thus here, as in the rest of the Bible, the moral life was seen as the foundation of the Jewish faith. Theology was defined in relation to practical activity; it was through ethical praxis that humanity encountered the Divine.

Rabbinic literature continued this emphasis on action. Convinced they were the authentic expositors of Scripture, the rabbis amplified biblical law. In their expansion of the commandments, rabbinic exegetes differentiated between the laws governing human relationships to God (*bain adam la makom*) and those that concerned human relationships to others (*bain adam le chavero*). As in the biblical period, rabbinic teachings reflected the same sense of the primacy of morality. Such texts as the following indicated rabbinic priority:

> He who acts honestly and is popular with his fellow creatures, it is imputed to him as though he had fulfilled the entire Torah.
>
> Hillel said: "What is hateful to yourself, do not do to your fellow man. This is the entire Torah, the rest is commentary."
>
> Better is one hour of repentance and good deeds in this world than the whole life of the world-to-come [Spero 1983, 56–57].

In the classic texts of Judaism then moral behavior was the predominant theme. By choosing the moral life, the Jew could help to complete God's work of creation. To accomplish this task the rabbis formulated an elaborate system of traditions, which were written down in the Mishnah, subsequently expanded in the Talmud, and eventually codified in the *Code of Jewish Law.* According to traditional Judaism, this expansion of the Pentateuchal Law was part of God's revelation. Both the Written Law (*Torah Shebikthav*) and the Oral Law (*Torah Shebe-'alpe*) were binding on Jews for all time.

> The Torah has been revealed from Heaven. This implies our belief that the whole of the Torah found in our hands this day is the Torah that was handed down by Moses and that it is all of divine origin. By this I mean that the whole of the Torah came unto him from before God in a manner which is metaphorically called speaking [Maimonides, as quoted in Jacobs 1964, 216].

This Torah embraced the Pentateuch as well as its traditional interpretation: orthodoxy maintained that God gave to Moses the laws in the Pentateuch as well as their explanations.

> The verse: "And I will give thee the tables of stone, and the Law and the commandment, which I have written that thou mayest teach them" (Ex. 24:12) means as follows: "The tables of stone" are the ten commandments; "the law" is the Pentateuch; "the commandment" is the Mishnah; "which I

have written" are the Prophets and the Hagiographa; "that thou mayest teach them" is the Gemara (Talmud). This teaches that all these things were given on Sinai [R. Levi b. Hama in the name of R. Simeon b. Laquish, in Jacobs 1964, 282].

Given this view of the Torah, Jews regarded the moral law as absolute and binding. In all cases the law was precise and specific; it was God's word made concrete in the daily life of the Jew. The commandment to love one's neighbors embraced all humanity. In the *Code of Jewish Law* the virtues of justice, honesty, and humane concern were regarded as central virtues of community life; hatred, vengeance, deceit, cruelty, and anger were condemned as antisocial. The Jew was instructed to exercise loving-kindness toward all: to clothe the naked, to feed the hungry, to care for the sick, and to comfort the mourner. By fulfilling these ethical demands, the Jewish people could help to bring about God's kingdom on earth, in which exploitation, oppression, and injustice would be eliminated. What was required in this task was a commitment to ethical praxis as a policy.

5. ORTHOPRACTICE VERSUS ORTHODOXY

In contrast to this emphasis on the centrality of moral praxis, the Jewish religion does not insist on the acceptance of formal theological dogma. Like liberation theology, the hallmark of the Jewish tradition is orthopraxis rather than theological orthodoxy. In the history of the Jewish faith there has never been a central body that took upon itself the responsibility of formulating a religious creed. The books of the Bible and early rabbinic literature contained numerous beliefs about God's nature and activity, yet neither the Bible nor the Mishnah contained a list of correct beliefs nor a commandment to believe in God. It was not until the Hellenistic period that there was an attempt to outline the articles of the Jewish faith.

Responding to views of his day that he believed to be against the spirit of the Jewish faith, the Jewish philosopher Philo formulated five principles that he felt Jews were bound to accept: God is eternal; God is One; the world was created; the world is One; God exercises forethought (see Jacobs 1964, 8-9.) It is noteworthy that these beliefs were conditioned by external circumstances; Philo did not examine the sources of Judaism in an objective manner to discover the basic principles of Judaism. His purpose was simply to highlight the ideas that needed to be stressed as principles of faith in his time in response to the external challenge to Jewish belief.

Only infrequently in the development of early rabbinic Judaism were there other attempts to categorize the essential principles of Judaism. Significantly such lists included action as well as belief. For the rabbis it was impossible to separate religious conviction from ethical demands. In the third century, for example, Rabbi Simlai declared that the Torah could be reduced to a number of principles as reflected in the teachings of various biblical personages. King David, he maintained, summarized the Torah in eleven essentials:

(1) He who walks blamelessly
(2) and does what is right
(3) and speaks truth from his heart
(4) and does not slander with his tongue,
(5) and does no evil to his friend,
(6) nor takes up a reproach against his neighbour
(7) in whose eyes a reprobate is despised,
(8) but who honours those who fear the Lord
(9) who swears to his own hurt and does not change,
(10) who does not put out his money at interest,
(11) and does not take a bribe against the innocent
[Ps 15:2-5]

Isaiah reduced the Torah to six principles:

(1) He who walks righteously
(2) and speaks uprightly
(3) who despises the gain of oppressions
(4) who shakes his hands, lest they hold a bribe
(5) who stops up his ears from hearing of bloodshed
(6) and shuts his eyes from looking upon evil [Is 33:15].

Micah reduced it to three principles:

(1) To do justice
(2) to love kindness,
(3) and to walk humbly with thy God [Mi 6:8].

Isaiah reduced the Torah to two principles:

(1) Keep justice
(2) Do righteousness [Is 56:1].

Amos reduced it to one:

(1) Seek me and live [Am 5:4]

As did Habbakuk:

(1) But the righteous shall live by his faith [Hab 2:4]

We can see that belief and action were inextricably interrelated. For Rabbi Simlai—as for others—the essence of Judaism lay in the practical expression of the Jews' adherence to God's moral demands (see Jacobs 1964, 10).

It was not until the Middle Ages, when Jewish scholars faced the challenge of Greek philosophical thought as well as Christianity and Islam, that they again felt it necessary to outline the essential theological features of their faith. As with Philo, the rabbis of this period attempted to defend Judaism and to dwell on what they perceived as its unique features in order to combat an external threat. The most important formulation was Maimonides's thirteen principles of the Jewish faith.[1] Here, as in Philo's list, the emphasis was on correct belief: only those who subscribed to these tenets were to be included in the general body of Israel (see Jacobs 1964, 17).

Other Jewish thinkers challenged Maimonides's formulation. Hasdai Crescas, for example, maintained that there was one basic belief, eight other important beliefs, eleven true opinions, and thirteen probabilities. Simon ben Zemah Duran argued that there were only three essential principles of the Jewish faith, which included by implication Maimonides's other principles. Similarly

Joseph Albo declared that there were three principles, eight derived beliefs, and six tenets, which everyone professing the Law of Moses was obliged to believe. Other scholars insisted that it was impossible to extract a set of principles from the Torah. Asked whether he accepted the formulations of Maimonides, Crescas, or Albo, David ben Soloman Ibn Abi Zimra stated: "I do not agree that it is right to make any part of the perfect Torah into a 'principle' since the whole Torah is a 'principle' from the Mouth of the Almighty" (Jacobs 1964, 24).

It was not surprising that there was such disagreement among rabbinic authorities since the classic texts of Judaism were essentially nonspeculative in character. Without an overall authority whose opinion in theological matters was binding on all Jews, it was inevitable that rabbinic opinion would conflict about such a central issue as the fundamental tenets of the faith. And without such a binding framework of religious belief, equally contentious discussions often arose over theological matters.

A major religious disagreement divided the Jewish community as early as the Hellenistic period. The Sadducees adhered to the literal meaning of Pentateuch and rejected the belief in an afterlife, whereas the Pharisees believed that the soul survived death and that God revealed the Oral as well as the Written Law. According to Josephus, the Pharisees

> believe that souls have power to survive death and that there
> are rewards and punishments under the earth for those who
> have led lives of virtue or vice. . . . The Sadduccees hold that
> the soul perishes along with the body. They own no observ-
> ances of any sort apart from the laws [as quoted in Bowker
> 1973, 89].

6. THEOLOGICAL DEBATE AND LATER JUDAISM

In later Judaism, Jewish thinkers continued to differ about fundamental matters. Maimonides argued that God should only be described by using negative attributes; to ascribe to God positive attributes, he believed, was a form of polytheism because it suggested that other beings, namely the divine attributes, were coexistent with God for all eternity. According to Maimonides, when we declared that God was one, we were not saying anything about God's true nature, but we were negating all plurality from the divine being. Positive attributes were permitted only if it was understood that they referred to God's actions rather than God's nature.

Hasdai Crescas disputed this claim. It was impossible, he contended, to avoid the use of positive attributes, and there was nothing offensive in using them since there was a real relationship between God and the world God had created, even though God was infinite and creatures finite. Another theory was put forward by the Kabbalists who distinguished between God *in se* and God as manifested to creatures. For the Kabbalists God was revealed through divine emanations, but God as God was the *En Sof.* Positive attributes, they maintained, were permissible in speaking of God as manifest; but of God as God, not even negative attributes were then allowed (Jacobs 1973, 43).

Jewish thinkers also had differing opinions concerning God's omniscience. According to Gersonides and Crescas, it was logically impossible for God to have foreknowledge and for human beings to have free will. For Gersonides, God knew things in general but was not omniscient. God did not know in advance what human beings would choose. Crescas, on the other hand, maintained that human beings were not free since all their actions were determined by God's foreknowlege. Maimonides held that God had foreknowledge and yet human beings were free. Human foreknowledge, Maimonides asserted, was incompatible with free will, but divine foreknowledge was fundamentally different from human knowledge. Therefore divine ominiscience was compatible with free will.

A similar debate concerned God's providence: Maimonides and Gersonides defended the doctrine of general providence and linked special providence to enlightened human beings. Only those who were excellent intellectually and morally, they asserted, came under God's special care. Hasidism extended the doctrine further. According to this view, divine providence was over everything since God was the creator of all. Nothing moved without God's causal action (Jacobs 1973, 78–79).

The problem of evil similarly exercised rabbinic authorities, and here too there were serious differences of opinion. Abraham Ibn

Daud maintained that God did not create evil since God was all good. What we conceived as evil, he explained, was actually an absence of good. It was therefore incorrect to say that God created evil; there was in reality no evil, only the absence of good. What could be said instead was that God did not create certain goods for particular people.

Maimonides's view was essentially the same: all evils were privations. Thus God did not create evil but was responsible for the privation of good. In Kabbalistic Judaism, evil was seen as positive. According to Lurianic doctrine, God withdrew from the Godhead into the Godhead to make room for the world. The light that moved into this space resulted in the "breaking of the vessels," and even after the reconstruction of the spheres, some light was poured over to form worlds of decreasing order until eventually it nourished the inhabitants of the evil realm. Evil was thus the result of a cosmic catastrophe (Jacobs 1973, 130).

Another rabbinic controversy concerned the resurrection of the dead. Saadia Gaon believed that the soul would be reunited with the body and both together would be rewarded or punished. Saadia believed that both reward and punishment were eternal. Only such limitless reward and punishment, he believed, would provide proper incentives for God's worship, and even eternal punishment was due to God's kindness in the divine desire to make human beings virtuous.

Maimonides's doctrine of the afterlife was essentially spiritual. There would be a resurrection of the body, but it would endure for only a short time. Ultimately it was the soul that was immortal in the world to come. Maimonides equated hell with the annihilation of the sinner's soul rather than with actual torment. Nahmanides argued that hell was an actual place. It would be unjust, he asserted, to have the same punishment for all the wicked regardless of the severity of their sins (Jacobs 1973, 310–314).

These rabbinic discussions illustrate that within mainstream Judaism there is great scope for individual interpretation. The theological views of individual teachers were their own opinions, enjoying only as much authority as the teachers' learning. All Jews are obliged to accept the divine origin of the Law, but this was not so with regard to the various theological concepts expounded by the rabbis. For this reason, many modern Jewish thinkers have felt justified in abandoning various elements of traditional rabbinic theology that they no longer regard as tenable. Traditional rabbinic eschatology, for example, has been largely replaced by belief in the immortality of the soul. The late chief rabbi of England, J.H. Hertz, for example, argued that what really mattered was the doctrine of the immortality of the soul.

> Many and various are the folk beliefs and poetic fancies in the rabbinic writings concerning Heaven, *Gan Eden*, and Hell, *Gehinnom*. Our most authorative religious guides, however, proclaim that no eye hath seen, nor can mortal fathom, what awaiteth us in the Hereafter; but that even the tarnished soul will not forever be denied spiritual bliss [Hertz, 258].

This flexibility of theological interpretation and doctrine was reflected in the traditional Jewish conversion procedure. The emphasis of Jewish conversion was on joining the community and accepting the Law, not on the convert's personal religious convictions. For this reason converts were told of the persecution and discrimination that Jews have endured. As members of the Jewish community, they might well suffer similar indignities. Further, converts were made aware of the legal obligations they must assume as Jews. The conversion ceremony was thus regarded as a legal rite of passage by which the converts would take their place within the community.

The religious framework of conversion was assumed; a declaration of willingness was required to become part of the Jewish people. Orthopraxis rather than theological orthodoxy was the requirement, as was explained in the *Code of Jewish Law*:

> When the would-be proselyte presents himself, he should be examined lest he be motivated to enter the congregation of Israel by hope of financial gain or social advantage or fear. . . . If no unethical motive is found, the candidate is told of the heaviness of the yoke of the Torah and how difficult it is for the average person to live up to the commandments of the Torah. This is done to give the candidate a chance to withdraw if he so desires. If the candidate goes through with

all this and is not dissuaded and it is apparent that his motives are of the best, he is accepted [Yoreh Deah, 268].

7. SUMMARY

We can see therefore that the Jewish tradition places Halakhic observance at its center. Though the Jewish faith is based on the belief in God's action in history and revelation of the Torah, individual theological speculation is not regarded as authoritative. The Law, as contained in the Pentateuch and expanded by the rabbis, is the basis of the religious system. As with liberation theology, action—in particular moral praxis—is at the heart of the faith. Of primary importance is the translation of religious conviction into concrete behavior in this world. God's truth is to be fulfilled by deeds of loving-kindness; according to both traditions, faith is the total human response to God. True faith is not a simple affirmation of abstract truths as formulated in a creed, but a commitment, an overall attitude, a particular posture to life. Faith in action—ethical praxis—is the truest expression of religious devotion, and in this both Judaism and liberation theology stand together in the quest for a better world.

CHAPTER SIX

Common Ground and Shared Concerns

1. LINKS BETWEEN JUDAISM AND
LIBERATION THEOLOGY

Despite the common ground we have explored there are important theological differences between Judaism and liberation theology. As in the past Jews today would regard the liberationist's adherence to traditional christology as misguided. For the Jew, God is an absolute unity; God is indivisible and unique, containing no plurality. Given this understanding, the doctrine of the Incarnation must be rejected. The belief that Jesus was both man and God continues to be considered a blasphemous heresy. Contemporary Jewish thinkers also reject trinitarianism in any form; there is simply no way to harmonize the belief in Jewish monotheism with the conception of a triune God. Similarly, Jews of all degrees of observance deny the liberationists' claim that Jesus was the Messiah. For Jews, Jesus did not fulfill the messianic expectations: he did not gather in the exiles and restore the Law; he did not rebuild the Temple; nor did he bring about a cataclysmic change in human history. Further, Jews deny that Jesus had an extraordinary relationship with God and that he can forgive sins.

Despite these differences, Jews can find much to sympathize with in liberation theology. As we have seen, liberationists focus on the flesh-and-blood Jesus of the gospels; they have reclaimed the historical context of the New Testament. Instead of analyzing Jesus' divine and human character, the facts of the ministry of Jesus provide

112

the basis for their theology. Like the prophets of the Old Testament, Jesus is seen as the conscience of Israel. Just as the ancient prophets criticized the people of Israel for their iniquity so did Jesus attack the scribes and Pharisees for their lack of righteousness. Given this understanding, it is possible for Jews to gain an appreciation of Jesus' mission.

Jesus' departure from Jewish Law should therefore not be construed as a rejection of Judaism itself, but as a critique of religious corruption and moral stagnation. In his confrontations with the leaders of the nation, Jesus echoed the words of the prophets by denouncing hypocrisy and injustice. The love of wealth and the exploitation of the poor, he contended, made it impossible to establish a proper relationship with God. It was his conviction that the leaders had led the people away from true worship of God; in his ministry Jesus opposed a life of ritual practice devoid of moral concern. As a prophetic figure Jesus should be recognizable to all Jews; like the prophets, he emphasized that loving-kindness is at the heart of the Jewish faith. Jesus' words thus recalled such figures as Amos, Hosea, Isaiah, and Jeremiah; he stood firmly within the Jewish tradition.

By concentrating on Jesus' prophetic role and ministry, liberation theologians have brought the temporal dimension into prominence. Putting into the background Christianity's otherworldly outlook, they stress that Christian action is of primary concern. The kingdom of God, they state, must be understood as intimately connected with the establishment of justice. As in Judaism, the kingdom is conceived by liberation theologians as taking place on the terrestrial plane. Jesus inaugurated the first stage in this process—the building of God's kingdom, which entails a total transformation of the old order through active struggle. By declaring the coming of the kingdom, Jesus was issuing a call to strive for the physical and spiritual liberation of the oppressed. Social structures must be changed if peace and justice are to be established. Such an understanding of Jesus' message is an important departure from traditional Christian thought; the emphasis on social realities rather than internal attitudes is a profound shift from the past.

This radical break with previous Christian conceptions of the kingdom is of crucial significance for the Jewish perception of liberation theology. Though Jews are unable to accept the claim that Jesus ushered in the period of messianic redemption, they can easily accept the liberationists' view that God wants everyone to take part in bringing about the kingdom of God. As we have seen, this understanding is a fundamental element of Old Testament theology and rabbinic thought; for Jews the kingdom of God consists of a complete moral order. The fulfillment of the conception ultimately rests with the Messiah, but it is humanity's duty to participate in the creation of a better society in anticipation of the messianic redemption. Throughout Jewish literature, Jews have been called to bring about the rule of truth and holiness. Thus for both Jews and liberation theologians the establishment of the kingdom of God is a process in which all human beings have an important role. The rejection of an internalized, spiritual, and otherworldly kingdom draws liberation theology back to its Jewish roots.

In this struggle to bring about God's kingdom, liberation theologians constantly look back to the history of the Jewish people for inspiration. Nowhere is this more apparent than in their use of the Exodus experience as a paradigm of liberation. In their exposition of the biblical account, liberationists emphasize that God was on the side of the afflicted. The Exodus event is of equal significance for the Jewish nation; for the Jews God is the Savior of the people. The Exodus experience is a core event in the self-understanding of the Jews. In Jewish sources and in the Passover liturgy, the deliverance from Egypt was seen as a symbol of freedom. Throughout the Passover meal Jews are admonished to remember that they were slaves in Egypt so that they will take sides with those persecuted today. Passover is not simply a festival commemorating a past occurrence. It is a perpetual reminder that human emancipation must take place everywhere. Jews and liberationists thus share a common heritage and vision of a future in which all humankind will be delivered from bondage.

In the account of the Exodus from Egypt, the faith of Israel was portrayed as a response to God's will. What was required of Israel was obedient participation in the act of emancipation. For liberation theologians this biblical anchorage leads to a practical orientation of the faith: praxis, rather than theological reflection, is understood as the key to Christian witness. Liberation theologians stress that theology must start from actions committed to the process of liberation; theology is a critical reflection on praxis.

For Jews the emphasis on the concrete dimension of faith is vital. The Jewish hope lies in God's rule on earth. This is the goal of the history of the world in which the Jewish people have a central role. Throughout the Bible and in rabbinic literature ethical behavior was the predominant theme. By doing God's will the Jew could help to complete the work of creation. As in liberation theology, the Jewish religion focuses on orthopraxis rather than theological orthodoxy. Theological speculation is not seen as authoritative; instead moral praxis is at the core of the faith. Deeds of goodness rather than dogma take precedence. Jews and Christian liberation theologians are thus united in the quest for the total elimination of human wickedness.

2. A MARXIST PERSPECTIVE

This shared vision can serve as a bridge between the two traditions. Liberation theology's return to traditional Jewish ideals should make it possible for both faiths to work together for the first time in areas of social concern. Liberation theologians have paved the way for such a common endeavor by explaining how ethical values rooted in the Bible can be put into practice. As we have seen in their analysis of society and in trying to understand conflict, liberation theologians frequently utilize the insights of Marxism. For liberation theologians Marxism is essentially an instrument of social analysis; the Marxist looks at the world and believes it is possible to understand the relationship between oppressor and oppressed.

In explaining this position, liberation theologians point out that they do not accept Marxism as an all-embracing framework in which themes such as dialectical materialism, the inevitability of historical struggle, or religion as the opiate of the people play a predominant role. Liberation theologians believe that the insights of Marxism can help them to understand the nature of exploitation; in this light class struggle is viewed as a dominant feature of modern life. To those who see life "from below," conflict between classes is a social reality in which major forces are polarized. To be oppressed means to be in a sitation of dependency; denied the opportunity of being architects of their own destiny, the weak are economically, politically, and culturally subservient.

In the past Christians tended to interpret evil in individualistic terms. For liberation theologians evil is systemic; it is embodied in the structures of society. The task of liberation theology is to engage in a restructuring of the social and economic order, and in this quest liberation theology articulates the aspirations of oppressed peoples and social classes.

> The theology of liberation attempts to reflect on the experience and meaning of the faith based on the commitment to abolish injustice and to build a new society; this theology must be verified by the practice of that comittment, by active, effective participation in the struggle which the exploited social classes have undertaken against their oppressors. Liberation from every form of exploitation is the possibility of a more human and more dignified life, the creation of a new man—all pass through this struggle [Gutiérrez 1973, 307].

In defending their adoption of a Marxist perspective, liberation theologians are anxious to demonstrate that Christianity has always borrowed from secular ideology and philosophical thought. In the past, they point out, Christianity has erected elaborate theoretical structures based on the writings of such thinkers as Plato, Aristotle, Hegel, and others. Thus, they argue, it should not seem strange that liberation theology contains features of Marxism.

The Jewish faith developed in similar fashion. Thus for Jews, the attempt to incorporate selected elements of Marxist social analysis into a theory of liberation should not be untenable as long as it is clear that there are important limits to such an adaptation. Full-fledged Marxism with its atheistic bias can find no place in a Jewish evaluation of society and its ills. But if Marxism is seen as an instrument of analysis—a tool of social science— there should be no objection to its being employed by Jews as a methodology for understanding oppression. Rather than distort the Jewish faith, the incorporation of a Marxist viewpoint in the social sphere can help to illuminate societal reality. In a spirit of cooperation and mutual concern then, united by a common heritage, Jews and Christians can set out on a mutual undertaking in a number of important areas to which liberation theology has already directed attention.

3. SOCIALISM

Liberation theologians have emphasized the importance of building a more socialist order. Recognizing the existence of class conflict, they advocate the abolition of its causes. In particular they seek to restructure the socioeconomic foundations of society. What is needed, they believe, is a more egalitarian structure. According to the body of liberationist priests who gathered together in Santiago (Chile) in April 1972, unbridled capitalism is responsible for numerous ills (Eagleson 1975, 3): marginal living and alienation, excessive inequality between different social classes, the continuing and increasing frustration of people's expectations; the unjust exercise of repressive power by dominant parties and rulers; tensions resulting from the dependence of countries on other centers of economic power, growing imbalance and perversion of international trade; the flight of economic and human resources; the evasion of taxes by various countries; rising indebtedness; international monopolies and the imperialism of money (Eagleson 1975, 100).

To escape from these evils, liberation theologians contend that a major transformation must take place. The Christian must press for the adoption of socialist principles and policies. Such a program would ideally result in a more equal distribution of goods and services. Facilities such as schools, hospitals, housing, subsidies for the ill and elderly, and employment opportunities would be available for all. By incorporating such values into the fabric of society, liberationists assert that it would no longer be possible for the few to maximize profit for themselves alone; instead the material benefits of labor would be spread throughout the community.

Many Jews today would welcome such reforms. No doubt they would reject both a full-fledged socialist state along Marxist-Leninist lines and violent revolution, but the infusion of socialist ideals into society would for a considerable number evoke a positive response. For these Jews the need to provide an adequate standard of living for everyone is of central importance. There is every reason to believe that such Jews—inspired by the social message of the Bible—could join ranks with liberation theologians in the quest for equality, justice, and unity. Drawing inspiration from their shared traditions they could subscribe to a political strategy that is uncompromising in giving priority to the urgent needs of all humankind.

4. THE POOR

At the heart of the desire to transform society is an identification with the poor. Liberation theologians stress that in the past Christians interpreted Jesus' words "Blessed are the poor, for yours is the kingdom of God" as meaning that one should accept poverty because injustice will be compensated for in the hereafter. Such an interpretation gives material poverty a positive value: it is understood as austerity and indifference to the things of this world. According to liberation theology this is a mistake. Poverty is not to be idealized; it must be seen for what it is—an evil to be abolished. Further, the existence of poverty is not a coincidence, but the result of greed.

It is intolerable because it contradicts the very purpose of God's mighty act of deliverance—to rescue his people from the slavery of Egypt. It robs man of his humanity as a steward and transformer of the world and it therefore contradicts the mandate of creation. . . . It breaks human solidarity and consequently it destroys friendship among men and with God [Míguez Bonino 1975, 112].

For liberation theologians the starting point of theological reflection is the poor, not abstract metaphysical theories; the view "from below" is essential. Liberation theology claims that God is to be found in the situation of the poor, just as in Scripture God is the savior of the enslaved. What is required then is solidarity as a protest against poverty. Gutiérrez explains that solidarity is a "way of identifying oneself with the interests of the oppressed classes and challenging the exploitation that victimized them" (Gutiérrez 1975, 14). Poverty is to be fought against and destroyed; God's salvation is achieved in the process of liberation. The problems and struggles of the poor are our own. The vocation of every person is to opt for human love and compassion. "Solidarity with the poor implies a commitment to turn human love into a collective experience from which there is no turning back" (Cusianovich 1979, 139).

As God's suffering servant through the ages, the Jewish people should find this message of solidarity with the poor of paramount significance. The prophets condemned every kind of abuse. Scripture speaks of positive action to prevent poverty from becoming widespread. Leviticus and Deuteronomy contain detailed legislation designed to prevent the accumulation of wealth and consequent exploitation of the unfortunate. Jews should thus feel an obligation to take steps to eradicate poverty and suffering from the modern world. In particular, they should address themselves to the economic deprivation that affects certain groups: the young, who are frustrated by the lack of opportunity to obtain training and work; manual laborers, who are frequently ill-paid and find difficulty in defending their rights; the unemployed, who are discarded because of the harsh exigencies of economic life; and the old, who are often marginalized and disregarded. In all such cases, the Jewish people—who have consistently endured hardship—should feel drawn to the downtrodden of modern society, sharing in their distress.

5. THE THIRD WORLD

In pleading the case of the poor, liberation theologians—who are predominantly Latin American—have focused on the plight of the oppressed in the third world. The underdevelopment of the poor countries, they point out, is the consequence of the development of other countries.

> The dynamics of the capitalist economy lead to the establishment of a center and a periphery, simultaneously generating progress and growing wealth for the few and social imbalances, political tensions, and poverty for the many [Gutiérrez 1973, 84].

The countries of Latin America were born into this context: they emerged as dependent societies in consequence of economic exploitation. Such unequal structures dominate and determine the character of the particular cultures of these countries, and they necessitate a defense of the status quo. Even modernization and the introduction of a greater rationality into the economies of these societies is required by the vested interests of the dominant groups. Imperialism and colonization are thus hallmarks of the past and present economic climate. From a cultural point of view as well, such imbalance between "developed" and "underdeveloped" countries is acute—the underdeveloped areas are always far away from the cultural level of the industrialized centers.

The perception of the fact of this dependence and its consequences has made it possible to formulate a policy of reform. According to liberation theology, human freedom cannot be brought about by a developmentalist approach that maintains elitism. Instead liberationists grapple with the existing relationship based on injustice in a global frame. By analyzing the mechanisms that are being used to keep the poor of the world under domination, liberation theologians assert that authentic development can only take place if the domination of the great capitalistic countries is eliminated. A transformation is needed to change radically the conditions in which the poor live. In this process, human beings assume conscious responsibility for their own destiny. Gutiérrez explains:

> This understanding provides a dynamic context and broadens the horizons of the desired social changes. In this perspective the unfolding of all of man's dimensions is demanded—a man who makes himself throughout his life and throughout history. The gradual conquest of true freedom leads to the creation of a new man and a qualitatively different society [Gutiérrez 1973, 36-37].

These themes of liberation and emancipation should have important echoes for the Jewish community. As we have seen, the biblical narrative portrays the ancient Israelites as an oppressed nation redeemed by God. Throughout history the Jewish people have been God's suffering servant—despised and rejected, smitten and afflicted. Through their suffering Jews gain a sympathetic awareness of the situation of others.

The lesson of the Passover is at the heart of Jewish aspirations for all peoples, as we read in the Passover liturgy:

> May He who broke Pharaoh's yoke forever shatter all fetters of oppression and hasten the day when sword shall, at last, be broken and wars ended. Soon may He cause the glad tidings of redemption to be heard in all lands, so that mankind—freed from violence and from wrong, and united in an eternal covenant of brotherhood—may celebrate the universal Passover in the name of our God of freedom [*Union Haggadah* 1923, 78].

In this spirit, it is possible for Jews to heed the plea of those who are downtrodden in the third world. Joining with liberationists, they can together press for a restructuring of the economic sphere. By combatting the worst elements of capitalism, it is possible for both Jews and Christians to participate in the struggle to bring about a better way of life.

6. FIRST WORLD CONCERNS

Preoccupation with the third world does not preclude concern for the oppressed in first world countries. Liberation theologians stress that grave inequalities between the rich and the poor also exist in the first world. Despite the higher general standard of living in these countries, many suffer substandard living conditions, poor health, concern about jobs, and constant worry about money.

> The epidemic rates of alcoholism and other forms of drug abuse, of rape, wife-beating, child abuse, and other forms of violence, of psychosomatic diseases like certain kinds of ulcers and heart disease, suggest the depths of anguish and alienation which many experience in our society [Cormie 1981b, 29].

Liberation theology points out two segments in the labor market: primary sector jobs with high wages, good working conditions, employment stability and job security, and secondary sector jobs with low wages, poor working conditions, harsh and arbitrary discipline, and little opportunity for advancement (Cormie 1981b, 33).

Consumerism is a dominant ideology that contributes to inequality. The most important questions deal with saving taxes and getting the best prices for goods.

> This attempt to focus our interests and life priorities on hairspray, cat food, and traveling to the Virgin Islands represents an assault on the One in whose image I am created. It is an assault on human dignity. Consumerism means that my eyes are offended, my ears are obstructed, and my hands are robbed of their creativity [Sölle 1981b, 9].

Exploitation in the first world is thus different from exploitation in third world countries. Inhabitants of the first world nations have become enmeshed in a cultural system that frequently perceives value in quantitative economic terms; the emphasis is on having rather than being. Such hedonistic tendencies—generated by fiercely competitive economic interests—divide the affluent from the poor.

Nowhere is this more apparant than in the Black community. In the United States, Cormie explains, slavery did not disappear with the disintegration of the plantation economy. After the Civil War most Blacks were relegated to work as sharecroppers. Even after the expansion of northern industries, most Blacks were channelled into the least desirable jobs and forced to live in dilapidated areas of the cities. Only a minority of Blacks have gained access to the privileges and status promised by the American dream (Cormie 1981b, 33).

Having once labored under the Egyptian yoke as slaves of Pharaoh, Jews today should be able to sympathize with the plight of such underprivileged sectors in the first world. In these countries, as in the countries of the third world, the gap between the rich and the poor needs to be bridged. In facing this challenge Jews should be able to unite with their liberationist sisters and brothers. The attempt to build a more just society should propel Jews into the vanguard of those who attempt to restructure institutions along more egalitarian lines. By putting themselves in the shoes of the disadvantaged, Jews can envisage what life must be for the under-privileged. In this way Jews together with liberationists can bring to the community policies of caring and sharing. This is theology "from below," from the standpoint of those who are neglected and marginalized. By bringing their suffering to bear on these problems, the Jewish community can make a major contribution to the redemption of the poor.

7. THE INNER CITY

In connection with first world poverty, liberation theology has focused on life in the inner city. Here the distinction between the powerful and the powerless is most clearly evident. In the cities—as opposed to the suburbs—are to be found the unemployed, families unable to cope, single parents, people with only part-time jobs, individuals on welfare, drop-outs, and recent immigrants. These are

> the people in the area of your town you don't go to, the place you pass through to get to a city or suburb, the place you keep your children away from, the place you pray for, thanking God you do not belong there [Vincent 1982, 17].

In such areas inhabitants are divorced from the powerful forces that shape their lives: the inner city is the place of failure and hopelessness. The graphic social divide between the rich and the poor is an everyday reality for those who live in large metropolitan centers. All too often the poverty of the inner city is the converse side of middle-class suburban life. The situation of the poor is an integral part of the elaborate hierarchy of wealth and esteem. The existence of rich suburbs is linked to the existence of ghettos and marginal sectors.

A new consciousness is needed to remedy this situation, an awareness of the calamities of inner-city deprivation. First-world theologians influenced by liberation theology contend that the proper Christian response is to engage in urban mission. By ministering to those at the bottom of society, Christians can affirm through their efforts that God is concerned with the plight of those facing adversity. Such activity constitutes an acted parable of the kingdom, bringing into focus the meaning of the gospel. Such a parable declares that the Christian cause is served best not by those in places of power and influence but by those in situations of vulnerability and powerlessness. According to liberationists, Christ is incarnate in the inner city. In his own time he belonged to the lower end of society; in today's world he is also to be found among the lowly. Urban mission thus aims to discover Jesus' message in the economic and cultural impoverishment of city life; from this vantage point, the Christian can strive to ameliorate the conditions of the downtrodden.

Jews too can enter into the life of the inner city in pursuit of this goal. Here they can embark on a task of reconstruction and restoration. Remembering their sojourn in the land of Egypt, they can identify with the impoverished; by going into the city, Jews can work alongside the poor for their betterment. The facts of the inner city demand commitment to change, and in this vocation liberationists can stand shoulder to shoulder with their Jewish sisters and brothers. Through urban mission Jews and Christians can affirm that hope for the modern world lies in a sympathetic response and dedication to the weak. Beginning at the grassroots, it is possible to work for the creation of a community in which all people can have a sense of pride and self-fulfillment. By laboring together in the neediest areas, the two faiths can join forces to bring about God's kingdom on earth.

8. THE UNEMPLOYED

As liberation theologians have noted, the unemployed are generally found in the destitute parts of the inner city. Unemployment is a growing problem. Liberationists have therefore directed attention to this deprived group. Gutiérrez, for example, stresses that the church has an obligation to those who are without work: they should be a focus of pastoral and theological activity. Christians must labor on behalf of the

underemployed and unemployed, who are dismissed because of the harsh exigencies of economic crises, and often because of development-models that subject workers and their families to cold economic calculations [Gutiérrez 1983, 134].

Such individuals face particular difficulties in coping with their misfortunes. The unemployed do not know what to do with their time, and as a consequence, they are unfulfilled in essential areas: basic human needs for human relationships, for financial income, for social status and identity, and for satisfaction and fulfillment.

Helping those faced with such difficulties should be a high priority. The Jewish community together with concerned Christians can take the lead in assisting those out of work. Recently Christian writers have made a number of suggestions about the kinds of activities that could be undertaken: ways must be sought for creating new work opportunities; labor not traditionally regarded as paid work (such as housework) must be accepted as valid and necessary; new manufacturing enterprises that stimulate the job market should be encouraged; apprenticeship for the young should be reintroduced; jobs need to be spread out through job sharing and part-time work; education must be seen as a preparation for life; voluntary activity should be stimulated and seen as a legitimate means of helping those in need (Handy 1983, 24–25).

In the quest to alleviate distress and disillusionment, Jews and Christians can make substantial contributions to those on the bottom of the social scale. Liberation from frustration and disappointment involves a reappraisal of life and labor: it is a task that can bind together both faiths in the quest for a meaningful life for all.

9. FEMINISM

Liberation theology has also been concerned about the plight of women. Feminist theologians have attempted to delineate the biblical traditions encapsulating the liberating experiences and visions of the people of Israel so as to help free women from oppressive sexist structures, instititions, and internalized values. In the view of these writers, women have been and continue to be socialized into subservient roles: either they are forced into domestic labor or they hold low-paying jobs. Only a few women manage to occupy jobs in traditionally male professions.

Work segregation is still the fundamental pattern of society. Women's work universally is regarded as of low status and prestige, poorly paid, with little security, generally of a rote and menial character. The sexist structuring of society means the elimination of women from those activities that allow for and express enhancement and development of the self, its artistic, intellectual and leadership capacities [Ruether 1983, 178].

Throughout society, these theologians maintain, the full humanity of woman is distorted, diminished, and denied.

To encourage the restoration of women's self-respect, liberationists focus on a number of biblical themes: God's defense and vindication of the oppressed; the criticism of the dominant systems of power; the vision of a new age in which iniquity will be overome; God's intended reign of peace. Feminist theology applies the message of the prophets to the situation of women; the critique of hierarchy thus becomes a critique of patriarchy. For these writers, images of God must include feminine roles and experiences, and language about God must be transformed. For Christians, they believe, it is necessary to move beyond a typology of Christ and the church that represents the dominant male and submissive female role. In Church structures women must be given full opportunities to participate at every level, including the ministry. In the civil sphere women must be granted full equality before the law—a stance that calls for the repeal of all discriminatory legislation. There must be equal pay for equal work and full access to all professions. Many liberationists also insist on women's right to reproduction, self-defense, sex education, birth control, and abortion as well as protecion against sexual harassment, wife-beating, rape, and pornography.

Similarly, in the Jewish community awareness of discrimination against women has been growing. Over the last two decades a significant number of Jewish feminists have attempted to restructure the position of women in traditional Judaism. In the past Jewish women were not directly involved with most Jewish religious activity. Today however Jewish women are trying to find ways to participate fully in their faith. In their attempt to reconcile Judaism and feminism these women are rediscovering various aspects of Jewish life: some study the place of women in Jewish history; others examine religious texts for clues to women's influence on Jewish life; still others redefine and feminize certain features of the Jewish tradition.

In seeking equality with men, these feminists demand that women be allowed to participate in the areas from which they have previously been excluded: serving as witnesses in a religious court, initiating divorce proceedings, being counted as part of a quorum for prayer, receiving rabbinic training and ordination, and qualifying as cantors. For these Jewish feminists, all formal distinctions in the religious as well as the secular sphere between men and women should be abolished.

> We have been trying to take charge of events in our own lives and in every area of what we call Jewish life: religion, the community, the family, and all our interpersonal relations [Schneider 1984, 19].

Given this impetus of liberating women from the restrictions of patriarchal structures, there is every reason for Jewish and Christian feminists to share their common concerns.

10. THE ENVIRONMENT

Not only do liberation theologians advocate a program of liberation for all humankind, they also draw attention to human responsibility for the environment: ecological liberation is an important element in their policy of emancipation. Since the scientific revolution, nature has been gradually secularized; no corner of the natural world has been untouched by human domination. Yet in this expansion of material productivity, the earth has been exploited to such a degree that pollution, famine, and poverty threaten humanity's very existence.

Liberationists assert that human beings must accept responsibility for the environment.

> The privilege of intelligence . . . is not a privilege to alienate and dominate the world without concern for the welfare of all other forms of life. On the contrary, it is the responsibility to become the caretaker and cultivator of the welfare of the whole ecological community upon which our existence de-

pends. . . . Although we need to remake the earth in a way
that converts our minds to nature's logic of ecological harmony, this will necessarily be a new synthesis, a new creation
in which human nature and nonhuman nature become
friends in the creating of a livable and sustainable cosmos
[Ruether 1983, 87–88, 91–92].

Reform in this area calls for a different attitude toward the
natural world; human beings must accept balance in nature as an
essential characteristic of the earth's ecosystem. Human intervention inevitably upsets the natural balance; thus steps must continually be taken to restore equilibrium to the earth. In particular,
environmentalists point out that care must be taken about the use
of pesticides. Habitations previously available to many living creatures have been destroyed; for agricultural purposes, we should
attempt to maintain diversity within nature and this requires a
careful monitoring of the use of chemical substances.

Pollution too is a major problem in the modern world; industry,
urban waste, and motor transport have all adversely affected the
environment, and conservationists maintain that adequate control
must be exercised over the use of pollutants that infect air and water
resources. Furthermore, environmentalists contend that human
beings must take steps to preserve endangered species and avoid
inflicting cruelty on wild and domestic animals.

The Jewish community has a role in all these endeavors. That
human beings are part of the ecological whole is fundamental to
Jewish thought. According to the Jewish faith, we have been given
authority over nature; such responsibility should curb the crude
exploitation of the earth for commercial purposes. The divine fiat
should foster in us a sympathetic understanding of the whole
ecological situation engendering for Jews as for Christians an
attitude of caring concern for all of God's creation.

11. SUMMARY

These then are some of the areas in which Jews can unite with
Christian liberation theologians to bring about God's kingdom. In
pursuit of the common goal of freedom from oppression, committed Jews and Christians can become a saving remnant of the
modern world, embodying the liberation message of Scripture.

Like Abraham they can hope against hope in laboring to build a more just and humane world. They can become an Abrahamic minority, attentive to the cry of oppression:

We are told that Abraham and other patriarchs heard the voice of God. Can we also hear the Lord's call? We live in a world where millions of our fellow men live in inhuman conditions, practically in slavery. If we are not deaf we hear the cries of the oppressed. Their cries are the voice of God. We who live in rich countries where there are always pockets of under-development and wretchedness, hear if we want to hear, the unvoiced demands of those who have no voice and no hope. The pleas of those who have no voice and no hope are the voice of God [Camara 1976, 16].

Throughout history the Jewish people have been God's suffering servant, yet inspired by a vision of God's reign on earth they have been able to transcend their own misfortunes in attempting to ameliorate the lot of others. In the contemporary world, where Jews are often comfortable and affluent, the prophetic message of liberation can too easily be forgotten. Liberation theology, however, with its focus on the desperate situation of those at the bottom of society, can act as a clarion call to the Jewish community, awakening the people of Israel to their divinely appointed task. Jewish tradition points to God's kingdom as the goal and hope of humankind: a world in which all peoples and nations shall turn away from iniquity and injustice. This is not the hope of bliss in a future life, but the building up of the divine kingdom of truth and peace among all peoples. "I will also give thee for a light to the nations, that my salvation may be unto the end of the earth" (Is 49:6).

In this mission the people of Israel and their Christian liberationist sisters and brothers can join ranks; championing the cause of the oppressed, afflicted, and persecuted, both faiths can unite in common cause and fellowship proclaiming together the ancient message of Jewish liturgy in their struggle to create a better world:

O Lord our God, impose Thine awe upon all Thy works, and let Thy dread be upon all Thou has created, that they may all form one single band to do Thy will with a perfect heart.

. . . Our God and God of our fathers, reveal Thyself in Thy splendor as King over all the inhabitants of the world, that every handiwork of Thine may know that Thou has made it, and every creature may acknowledge that Thou has created it, and whatsoever hath breath in its nostrils may say: the Lord God of Israel is King, and His dominion ruleth over all.

Jesus put it more concisely:

Thy Kingdom come,
thy will be done on earth as it is in heaven.

Notes

INTRODUCTION

1. Miranda's use of prophetic material is explained by R. M. Brown in *Theology in a New Key* (1978), 91.

CHAPTER ONE

1. In this chapter I have frequently used Weiss-Rosmarin, *Judaism and Christianity* (1965); Jacobs, *A Jewish Theology* (1973); Jacobs, *Principles of the Jewish Faith* (1964); and Silver, *Where Judaism Differed* (1956).

2. As formulated by Maimonides in his thirteen principles of the Jewish faith, *Commentary to the Mishnah Sanhedrin*.

CHAPTER TWO

1. See Works Cited for names of works by these authors.

2. See Miranda 1983 for a discussion of these issues.

3. See Miranda 1983 for a refutation of objections to the view that the wealthy must give away their riches.

CHAPTER THREE

1. The following discussion of Jewish ethics relies heavily on S. Spero, *Halakha in the Jewish Tradition* (New York, 1983).

CHAPTER FOUR

1. The prayers that follow are from the Haggadah. See C. Roth, *The Haggadah* (Israel).

2. *The Passover Anthology* by P. Goodman (Philadelphia: Jewish Publication Society, 1961) has been used as a source for Jewish literature about the Passover.

CHAPTER FIVE

1. (1) Belief in one God; (2) Belief in God's unity; (3) Belief in God's immortality; (4) Belief in God's eternity; (5) Belief that God alone is to be worshipped; (6) Belief in prophecy; (7) Belief that Moses was the greatest prophet; (8) Belief that the Torah was given by God to Moses; (9) Belief that the Torah is immutable; (10) Belief that God knows the thoughts and deeds of man; (11) Belief that God rewards and punishes; (12) Belief in the Messiah; (13) Belief in the resurrection of the dead.

Works Cited

Ahad Ha-Am. 1946. *Essays, Letters, Memoirs.* Ed. L. Simon. Oxford.

Assmann, Hugo. 1975. *Practical Theology of Liberation.* Tunbridge Wells, Kent (England): Search Press.

Atkinson, J. 1969. In Richardson 1969.

Balasuriya, Tissa. 1979. *The Eucharist and Human Liberation.* London: SCM Press. (Also published by Orbis Books as *Theology for a Nomad Church.* Maryknoll, N.Y.: Orbis Books 1979.)

Bigo, Pierre. 1977. *The Church and Third World Revolution.* Trans. Jeanne Marie Lyons. Maryknoll, N. Y.: Orbis Books.

Boff, Leonardo. 1978. *Jesus Christ Liberator.* Trans. Patrick Hughes. Maryknoll, N.Y.: Orbis Books.

———. 1980. "Christ's Liberation via Oppression." In Gibellini 1980.

Bowker, John. 1973. *Jesus and the Pharisees.* Cambridge (England): Cambridge University Press.

Brown, Robert M. 1978. *Theology in a New Key: Responding to Liberation Themes.* Philadelphia: Westminster.

Camara, Dom Helder. 1976. *The Desert Is Fertile.* New York: Jove Publications. (Also Maryknoll, N.Y.: Orbis Books, 1974, 1981.)

Cormie, L. 1981a. "The Challenge of Liberation Theology." In Richesin and Mahan 1981.

———. 1981b. "Liberation and Salvation." In Richesin and Mahan 1981.

Croatto, J. Severino. 1981. *Exodus.* Maryknoll, N.Y.: Orbis Books.

Cussianovich, Alejandro. 1979. *Religious Life and the Poor: Liberation Theology Perspectives.* Trans. John Drury. Dublin: Gill and Macmillan. (Also Maryknoll, N.Y.: Orbis Books 1979.)

Davies, J. G. 1976. *Christians, Politics and Violent Revolution.* Maryknoll, N.Y.: Orbis Books.

Dussel, Enrique. 1976. *History and the Theology of Liberation.* Maryknoll, N.Y.: Orbis Books.

Eagleson, John, ed. 1975. *Christians and Socialism.* Maryknoll, N.Y.: Orbis Books.

Echegoyen, M. 1971. "Priests and Socialism in Chile." *New Blackfriars* 52, 464 ff.

133

Ellacuría, Ignacio. 1976. *Freedom Made Flesh.* Trans. John Drury. Maryknoll, N.Y.: Orbis Books.

Fierro, Alfredo. 1977. *The Militant Gospel.* Trans. John Drury. Maryknoll, N. Y.: Orbis Books.

Finkelstein, L. 1942. *Haggadah of Passover.* New York.

Formstecher, Salomon. [1841] 1980. *Die Religion des Geistes.* Frankfurt: Ayer Co.

Gaon, Saadya. 1946. *The Book of Doctrines and Beliefs.* Trans. A. Altmann.

———. 1948. *The Book of Beliefs and Opinions.* Trans. S. Rosenblatt. New Haven.

Gibellini, Rosino, ed. 1980. *Frontiers of Theology in Latin America.* Trans. John Drury. London: SCM Press. (Also Maryknoll, N.Y.: Orbis Books, 1979.)

Glatzer, M. 1953. *Franz Rosenzweig: His Life and Thought.* New York.

Goodman, Philip, ed. 1961. *The Passover Anthology.* Philadelphia: Jewish Publication Society.

Gutiérrez, Gustavo. 1973. *A Theology of Liberation.* Trans. Sr. Caridad Inda and John Eagleson. Maryknoll, N.Y.: Orbis Books.

———. 1975. "Liberation Praxis and Christian Faith." In Gibellini 1980.

———. 1983. *The Power of the Poor in History.* Trans. Robert Barr. London (Also Maryknoll, N. Y.: Orbis Books, 1983.)

Halevi, Jehudah. [1927] 1964. *The Kuzari.* New York: Schocken.

Handy, C. 1983. "The Future of Work." *Christian* 8, 24–25.

Hertz, J. H. *Commentary to the Prayerbook.*

Heschel, Abraham J. [1955] 1969–1971. *The Prophets.* 2 vols. New York: Harper and Row.

Hick, John. 1974. *God and the Universe of Faiths.* New York: St. Martin's Press.

Jacobs, Louis. 1964. *Principles of the Jewish Faith.* London: Vallentine, Mitchell.

———. 1973. *A Jewish Theology.* New York: Behrman.

Jacobs, W. 1974. *Christianity through Jewish Eyes.* Cincinnati: HUC Press.

Joseph, M. 1903. *Judaism as Creed and Life.* London: Macmillan.

Klausner, J. 1956. *The Messianic Idea in Israel.* London: George Allen and Unwin.

Kohler, K. [1918] 1968. *Jewish Theology.* New York: Ktav.

Lazarus, M. 1900. *The Ethics of Judaism.* Philadelphia: Jewish Publication Society.

Míguez Bonino, José. 1975. *Doing Theology in a Revolutionary Situation.* Philadelphia: Fortress.

Miranda, José P. 1974. *Marx and the Bible.* Maryknoll, N.Y.: Orbis Books.

————. 1983. *Communism in the Bible*. London: SCM Press. (Also Maryknoll, N.Y.: Orbis Books, 1982.)

Patai, R. 1979. *The Messiah Texts: Jewish Legends of Three Thousand Years*. Detroit: Wayne State University Press.

Pérez-Esclarín, Antonio. 1978. *Atheism and Liberation*. Trans. John Drury. Maryknoll, N.Y.: Orbis Books.

Pixley, George V. 1981. *God's Kingdom: A Guide for Biblical Study*. Trans. Donald E. Walsh. Maryknoll, N.Y.: Orbis Books.

Richardson, Alan, ed. 1969. *A Dictionary of Christian Theology*. London: SCM Press.

Richesin, L. Dale, and Brian Mahan, eds. 1981. *The Challenge of Liberation Theology: A First World Response*. Maryknoll, N. Y.: Orbis Books.

Rosenzweig, Franz. 1930. *Der Stern der Erlosung*. Heidelberg.

————. 1953. *The Star of Redemption*. In N. Glatzer, *Franz Rosenzweig: His Life and Thought*. (New York).

Rubenstein, Richard. 1966. *After Auschwitz*. New York.

Ruether, Rosemary R. 1983. *Sexism and God-Talk*. Boston: Beacon Press.

Sandmel, Samuel. 1965. *We Jews and Jesus*. New York: Oxford University Press.

Schechter, Solomon. 1961. *Aspects of Rabbinic Theology: Major Concepts of the Talmud*. New York: Schocken.

Schneider, Susan. 1984. *Jewish and Female*. New York: Simon and Schuster.

Schoeps, Hans J. 1961. *Paul: The Theology in the Light of Jewish Religious History*. Trans. Harold Knight. Philadelphia: Westminster.

————. 1963. *The Jewish-Christian Argument*. London.

Segundo, Juan L. 1976. *The Liberation of Theology*. Trans. John Drury. Maryknoll, N.Y.: Orbis Books.

Silver, A. H. 1956. *Where Judaism Differed*. London.

Sobrino, Jon. 1978. *Christology at the Crossroads*. Trans. John Drury. Maryknoll, N.Y.: Orbis Books.

Sölle, Dorothee. 1981a. *Choosing Life*. London: SCM Press.

————. 1981b. "Liberation in a Consumerist Society." In Richesin and Mahan 1981.

————. 1981c. "Thou Shalt Have No Jeans Before Me." In Richesin and Mahan 1981.

Spektor, I. *Nachal Yitzchak*. In Spero 1983a, 134.

Spero, S. 1983. *Morality, Halakha and the Jewish Tradition*. New York: Ktav.

Steinham, Salomon Ludwig. 1863. *Die Offenbarungs lehre nach dem Lehrbegriff der Synagogue*. Leipzig.

Topel, John. 1979. *The Way to Peace: Liberation through the Bible.* Maryknoll, N. Y.: Orbis Books.

Troki, Isaac. 1975. *Faith Strengthened.* Trans. Moses Mocatta. New York: Hermon.

The Union Haggadah (USA). 1923.

Vermes, Geza. 1981. *Jesus the Jew.* Glasgow.

Vincent, John J. 1982. *Into the City.* London: Epworth Press.

Weiss-Rosmarin, Trude. 1965. *Judaism and Christianity: The Differences.* New York: Jonathan David.

Williams, A. L. 1939. *The Doctrines of Modern Judaism Considered.*